Tablet Covers

Accessorize your e-reader or tablet with personality! Great for gifts, too, these covers are made using quilter's fat quarters in exciting prints. They come in a variety of styles and four sizes to fit the most popular devices. Please refer to the finished measurements to find the best cover for your device.

LEISURE ARTS, INC.
Little Rock, Arkansas

EDITORIAL STAFF
Vice President of Editorial: Susan White Sullivan
Creative Art Director: Katherine Laughlin
Special Projects Director: Susan Frantz Wiles
Director of E-Commerce Services: Mark Hawkins
Technical Editor: Lisa Lancaster
Technical Writer: Jean Lewis
Art Category Manager: Lora Puls
Graphic Artists: Kara Darling,
   Becca Snider Tally, and Jessica Bramlett
Prepress Technician: Stephanie Johnson
Contributing Photographer: Mark Mathews
Contributing Photo Stylist: Christy Myers
Manager of E-Commerce: Robert Young

BUSINESS STAFF
President and Chief Executive Officer:
   Rick Barton
Vice President of Finance: Fred F. Pruss
Vice President of Sales-Retail Books: Martha Adams
Vice President of Mass Market: Bob Bewighouse
Vice President of Technology and Planning:
   Laticia Mull Dittrich
Director of Corporate Planning: Anne Martin
Information Technology Director:
   Brian Roden
Controller: Tiffany P. Childers
Senior Vice President of Operations: Jim Dittrich
Retail Customer Service Manager:
   Stan Raynor

We have made every effort to ensure that these instructions are accurate and complete. We cannot, however, be responsible for human error, typographical mistakes, or variations in individual work.

Copyright © 2013 by Leisure Arts, Inc., 5701 Ranch Drive, Little Rock, AR 72223, www.leisurearts.com. All rights reserved. This publication is protected under federal copyright laws. Reproduction or distribution of this publication or any other Leisure Arts publication, including publications which are out of print, is prohibited unless specifically authorized. This includes, but is not limited to, any form of reproduction or distribution on or through the Internet, including posting, scanning, or e-mail transmission.
Made in U.S.A.

Library of Congress Control Number: 2013944414

ISBN-13: 978-1-4647-1262-3

Meet Sue Marsh

As much as she loves everything about quilting, Sue Marsh of Whistlepig Creek Productions also has a soft spot for technology. Before going full-time in 1997 with her passion for designing quilt projects and fabrics, she worked in the petroleum industry.

"I am an engineer by education and a software developer by experience. I love technology and wouldn't/couldn't do my job without software and computerized equipment at my fingertips. The automation takes the tedium out of design and allows me to do the fun stuff."

She especially loves the tools, gadgets, and equipment that are available to quilters. "My house is stuffed with sewing, embroidery, and quilting machines. Plus fabric. Plus thread. Plus patterns. Plus, plus, plus…."

Knowing this about Sue, it's not surprising to hear that her favorite quote is, "If it's worth doing, it's worth doing to excess."

She describes her style as "Random! I like a little bit of everything. My fabric design has been whimsical, with a focus on kids. I've got a couple lines in the works that are modern and good for bag-making."

Bags and "smallish quilts" are Sue's preferred projects. "I really enjoy a project that comes together in a short amount of time, as I lose focus quickly. I am always more interested in the next project than the current one."

Sue has been sewing since the age of 12. "I did my first quilt project from a Quilt in a Day book. I literally made a king-size quilt in a day, and I was hooked."

She draws, sews, and quilts at the home she shares with her husband, Bernie, and five cats in a suburb of Denver, Colorado. For more about Sue and Whistlepig Creek Productions, visit her pages on Facebook, Pinterest, and wpcreek.blogspot.com.

CONTENTS

4 10 15
iPads

20 25 30
e-Readers

34 40 44
small e-Readers

48 53 58
mini e-Readers

General Instructions page 62

iPad
Cover 1

For iPad, iPad2, iPad 3rd and 4th generations, and other tablets measuring approximately 7½" x 9½" (19 cm x 24 cm). This version features an asymmetrical curved flap embellished with three large buttons.

Finished Cover Size (closed): approx. 8" x 10" x ½" (20 cm x 25 cm x 1 cm)
Finished Cover Size (open): approx. 22½" x 10" (57 cm x 25 cm)

4   www.leisurearts.com

SHOPPING LIST

Fat quarters are approximately 22" x 18" (56 cm x 46 cm).

- ☐ 2 coordinating fat quarters*
- ☐ 1 yd (91 cm) of 20" (51 cm) wide fusible woven interfacing such as Pellon® Shape-Flex® SF 101
- ☐ ¾ yd (69 cm) of 20" (51 cm) wide sew-in stiff stabilizer such as Pellon® Peltex® 70 Sew-In Ultra Firm Stabilizer
- ☐ Two 4½" (11 cm) lengths of ¾" (19 mm) wide elastic
- ☐ 1½" (4 cm) of ¾" (19 mm) wide hook and loop fastener
- ☐ Three 1¼" (32 mm) dia. buttons
- ☐ Removable fabric marking pen or pencil
- ☐ Tracing paper

* For directional prints you will need 1 additional fat quarter #2.

CUTTING THE PIECES

Refer to Cutting Diagrams, below, to cut fabric. All measurements include ¼" seam allowances. Flap patterns #1a & 1b are on pages 8-9.

From fat quarter #1:
- Cut 1 **outer cover** 17" x 10½".
- Cut 1 **pocket** 10½" x 5½".
- Cut 2 **corner squares** 3" x 3".

From fat quarter #2:
- Cut 1 **small lining** 8½" x 10½".
- Cut 1 **large lining** 9" x 10½".
- Cut 1 **flap** and 1 **flap lining reversed** from flap #1 pattern.

From fusible woven interfacing:
- Cut 1 **interfacing outer cover** 17" x 10½".
- Cut 1 **interfacing small lining** 8½" x 10½".
- Cut 1 **interfacing large lining** 9" x 10½".
- Cut 1 **interfacing flap** and 1 **interfacing flap lining reversed** from flap #1 pattern.

From stiff stabilizer:
- Cut 1 **base** 22½" x 10".

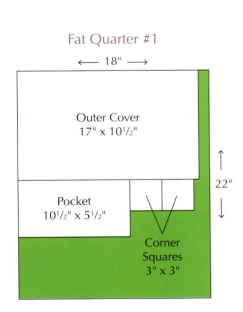

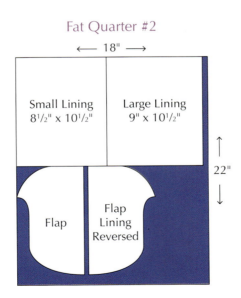

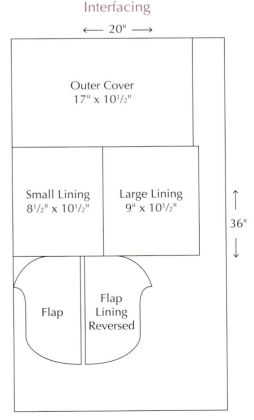

MAKING THE LINING

*Follow **Piecing**, page 63, and **Pressing**, page 64, to make the cover. Use ¼" seam allowances throughout.*

1. Following manufacturer's instructions, fuse each **interfacing lining** piece to wrong side of each corresponding fabric **lining** piece.

2. Fold and press each **corner square** in half diagonally to make 2 **corner triangles** *(Fig. 1)*.

Fig. 1

3. Matching raw edges, pin 1 corner triangle to each lower corner of **small lining**. Pin 1 elastic length to each upper corner. Using a scant ¼" seam allowance, baste triangles and elastic lengths to lining *(Fig. 2)*. Trim elastic even with edges of lining.

Fig. 2

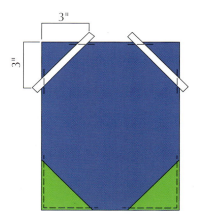

4. For the pocket, match wrong sides and press **pocket** in half lengthwise. Matching raw edges, pin pocket to left edge of **large lining**. Using a scant ¼" seam allowance, baste pocket to lining along three outer edges. Spacing as desired (ours are approximately 2½" apart), sew from fold to raw edge to divide pocket *(Fig. 3)*.

Fig. 3

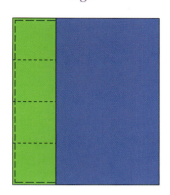

5. Sew large lining, small lining, and **flap lining** together *(Fig. 4)*. Press seams away from small lining. Using fabric marker, draw a line ½" from each seam. Press short raw edge ¼" to the wrong side.

Fig. 4

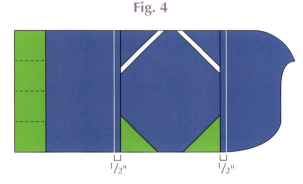

MAKING THE COVER

1. Fuse **interfacing flap** and **interfacing outer cover** to wrong side of each corresponding fabric piece.

2. Sew **outer cover** and **flap** together *(Fig. 5)*. Sew one piece of hook and loop fastener to right side of outer cover. Press short raw edge ¼" to the wrong side.

Fig. 5

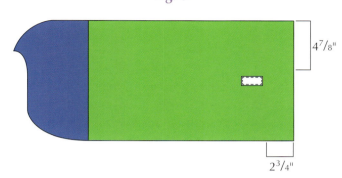

3. Unfolding pressed edges, sew outer cover and lining together *(Fig. 6)*. Trim seams and clip curves and point. Turn cover right side out, pushing out curves and point with a chopstick or skewer; press.

Fig. 6

4. To shape flap end of **base**, trim flap pattern along dashed lines. Draw around curved edge of pattern on one end of base *(Fig. 7)*; cut along drawn line.

Fig. 7

5. Slide base into cover and align outer seams with edges of base; press. *Note:* It will be a tight fit and you may have to slightly curl the base to slide it into the cover.

6. Stitch in the ditch along the vertical seams. Stitch on drawn lines. Refold pressed edges to the wrong side. Topstitch around entire cover, closing open edges in stitching *(Fig. 8)*.

Fig. 8

7. Stitching through all layers, sew remaining hook and loop fastener piece to lining side of flap where indicated in **Fig. 9**. Spacing as desired, sew buttons to right side of flap.

Fig. 9

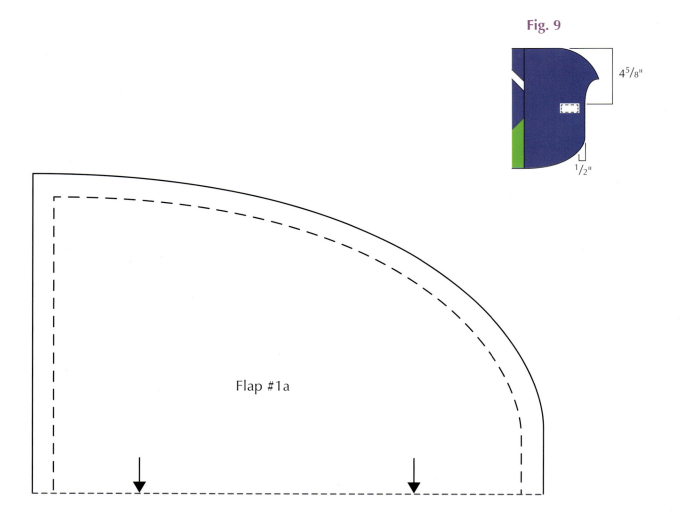

Flap #1a

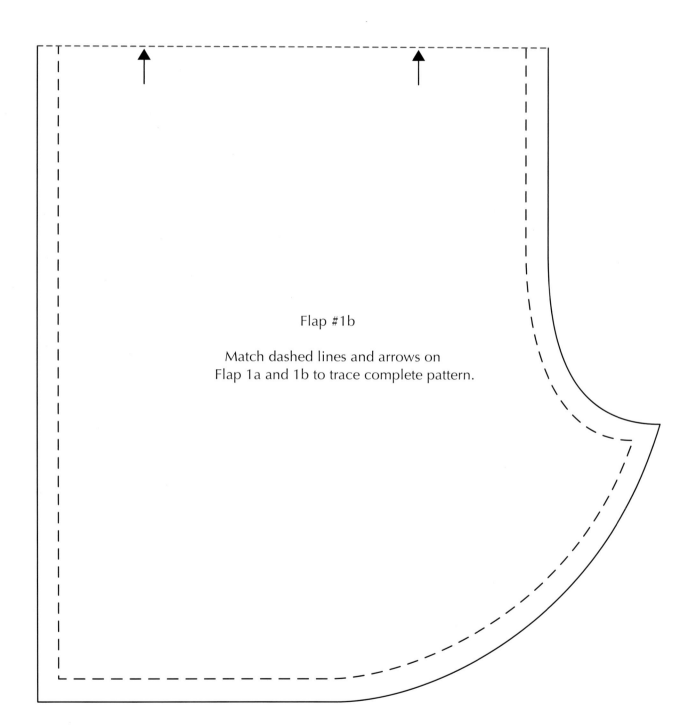

iPad
Cover 2

For iPad, iPad2, iPad 3rd and 4th generations, and other tablets measuring approximately 7$\frac{1}{2}$" x 9$\frac{1}{2}$" (19 cm x 24 cm). This version features a pieced outer cover and a rounded flap with layered buttons.

Finished Cover Size (closed): approx. 8" x 10" x $\frac{1}{2}$" (20 cm x 25 cm x 1 cm)
Finished Cover Size (open): approx. 22$\frac{1}{2}$" x 10" (57 cm x 25 cm)

SHOPPING LIST

Fat quarters are approximately 22" x 18" (56 cm x 46 cm).

- ☐ 2 fat quarters #1 (black dot)
- ☐ 1 fat quarter #2 (black print)*
- ☐ 1 fat quarter #3 (red tone-on-tone)
- ☐ 1 yd (91 cm) of 20" (51 cm) wide fusible woven interfacing such as Pellon® Shape-Flex® SF 101
- ☐ $\frac{3}{4}$ yd (69 cm) of 20" (51 cm) wide sew-in stiff stabilizer such as Pellon® Peltex® 70 Sew-In Ultra Firm Stabilizer
- ☐ Two 4$\frac{1}{2}$" (11 cm) lengths of $\frac{3}{4}$" (19 mm) wide elastic
- ☐ 1$\frac{1}{2}$" (4 cm) of $\frac{3}{4}$" (19 mm) wide hook and loop fastener
- ☐ 2$\frac{1}{8}$" (54 mm) dia. button
- ☐ 1$\frac{1}{8}$" (29 mm) dia. button
- ☐ Removable fabric marking pen or pencil
- ☐ Tracing paper

* For directional prints you will need 1 additional fat quarter #2.

www.leisurearts.com

CUTTING THE PIECES

*Refer to **Cutting Diagrams**, right, to cut fabric. All measurements include 1/4" seam allowances. Flap #2 pattern is on page 14.*

From fat quarters #1:
- Cut 1 **outer cover center strip** 17" x 3 1/2".
- Cut 1 **small lining** 8 1/2" x 10 1/2".
- Cut 1 **large lining** 9" x 10 1/2".
- Cut 1 **flap** and 1 **flap lining** from flap #2 pattern.

From fat quarter #2:
- Cut 2 **outer cover strips** 17" x 3 1/2".
- Cut 1 **pocket** 12 1/2" x 6 1/2".
- Cut 2 **corner squares** 3" x 3".

From fat quarter #3:
- Cut 2 **outer cover accent strips** 17" x 1".

From fusible woven interfacing:
- Cut 1 **interfacing outer cover** 17" x 10 1/2".
- Cut 1 **interfacing small lining** 8 1/2" x 10 1/2".
- Cut 1 **interfacing large lining** 9" x 10 1/2".
- Cut 1 **interfacing flap** and 1 **interfacing flap lining** from flap #2 pattern.

From stiff stabilizer:
- Cut 1 **base** 22 1/2" x 10".

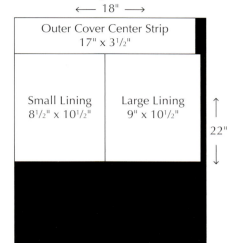
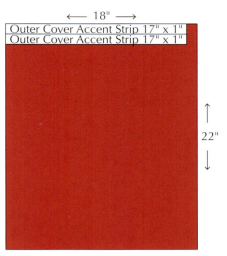
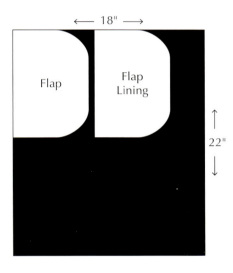
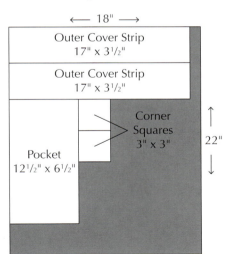
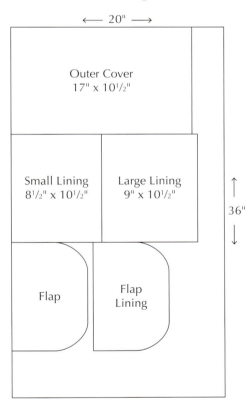

MAKING THE LINING

*Follow **Piecing**, page 63, and **Pressing**, page 64, to make the cover. Use 1/4" seam allowances throughout.*

1. Following manufacturer's instructions, iron each **interfacing lining** piece to wrong side of each corresponding fabric **lining** piece.

2. Fold and press each **corner square** in half diagonally to make 2 **corner triangles** *(Fig. 1)*.

Fig. 1

3. Matching raw edges, pin 1 corner triangle to each lower corner of **small lining**. Pin 1 elastic length to each upper corner. Using a scant 1/4" seam allowance, baste triangles and elastic lengths to lining *(Fig. 2)*. Trim elastic even with edges of lining.

Fig. 2

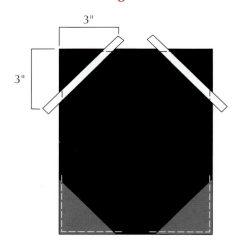

4. For the pocket, match right sides and short edges and fold **pocket** in half. Leaving an opening along bottom edge, sew around raw edges of pocket *(Fig. 3)*; clip corners, turn right side out, and press. Referring to **Fig. 4**, topstitch pocket to **large lining**.

Fig. 3

Fig. 4

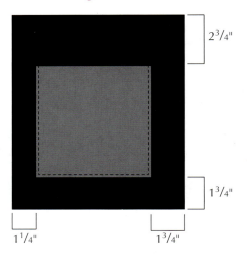

5. Sew large lining, small lining, and **flap lining** together *(Fig. 5)*. Press seams away from small lining. Using fabric marker, draw a line 1/2" from each seam. Press short raw edge 1/4" to the wrong side.

Fig. 5

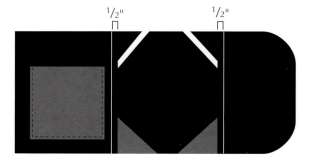

MAKING THE COVER

1. Sew **outer cover strips**, **outer cover center strip**, and **outer cover accent strips** together to make **outer cover** *(Fig. 6)*.

Fig. 6

2. Fuse **interfacing flap** and **interfacing outer cover** to wrong side of each corresponding fabric piece.

3. Sew **outer cover** and **flap** together *(Fig. 7)*. Sew 1 piece of hook and loop fastener to right side of outer cover. Press short raw edge ¼" to the wrong side.

Fig. 7

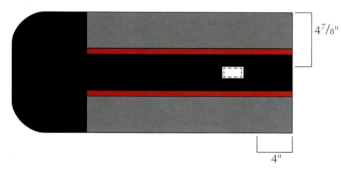

4. Unfolding pressed edges, sew outer cover and lining together *(Fig. 8)*. Trim seams and clip curves. Turn cover right side out, pushing out curves with a chopstick or skewer; press.

Fig. 8

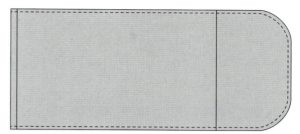

5. To shape flap end of **base**, trim flap pattern along dashed lines. Draw around pattern on one end of base; cut along drawn line *(Fig. 9)*.

Fig. 9

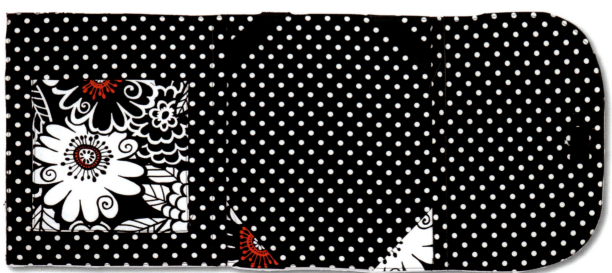

13

6. Slide base into cover and align outer seams with edges of base; press. ***Note:*** It will be a tight fit and you may have to slightly curl the base to slide it into the cover.

7. Stitch in the ditch along the vertical seams. Stitch on drawn lines. Refold pressed edges to the wrong side. Topstitch around entire cover, closing open edges in stitching *(Fig. 10)*.

8. Stitching through all layers, sew remaining hook and loop fastener piece to lining side of flap where indicated in **Fig. 11**. Spacing as desired, sew buttons to right side of flap.

Fig. 11

Fig. 10

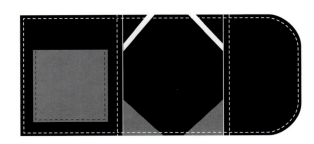

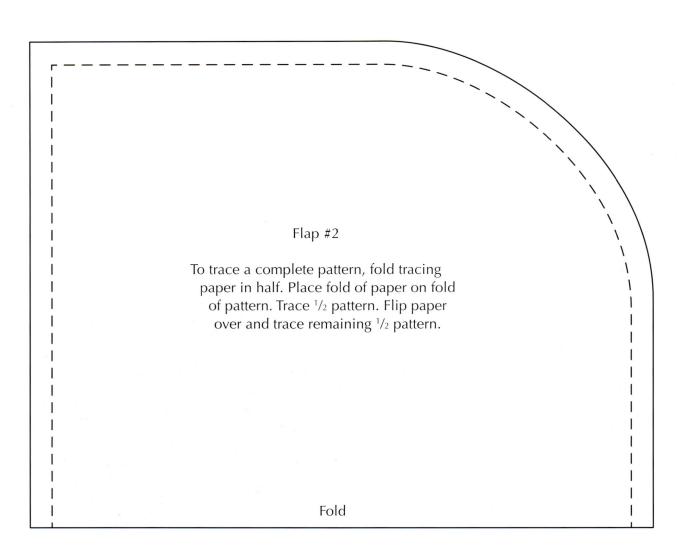

Flap #2

To trace a complete pattern, fold tracing paper in half. Place fold of paper on fold of pattern. Trace ½ pattern. Flip paper over and trace remaining ½ pattern.

Fold

iPad
Cover 3

For iPad, iPad2, iPad 3rd and 4th generations, and other tablets measuring approximately 7½" x 9½" (19 cm x 24 cm). This version features a pieced outer cover with a contrasting rectangular flap. Layered buttons accent the triangular tab.

Finished Cover Size (closed): approx. 8" x 10" x ½" (20 cm x 25 cm x 1 cm)
Finished Cover Size (open): approx. 22½" x 10" (57 cm x 25 cm)

SHOPPING LIST

Fat quarters are approximately 22" x 18" (56 cm x 46 cm).

- ☐ 1 fat quarter #1 (grey print)
- ☐ 2 fat quarters #2 (black/tan print)
- ☐ 1 fat quarter #3 (black speckled print)
- ☐ 1 yd (91 cm) of 20" (51 cm) wide fusible woven interfacing such as Pellon® Shape-Flex® SF 101
- ☐ ¾ yd (69 cm) of 20" (51 cm) wide sew-in stiff stabilizer such as Pellon® Peltex® 70 Sew-In Ultra Firm Stabilizer

- ☐ Two 4½" (11 cm) lengths of ¾" (19 mm) wide elastic
- ☐ 1½" (4 cm) of ¾" (19 mm) wide hook and loop fastener
- ☐ 2⅛" (54 mm) dia. button
- ☐ ⅞" (22 mm) dia. button
- ☐ Removable fabric marking pen or pencil

CUTTING THE PIECES
*Refer to **Cutting Diagrams**, below, to cut fabric.*
All measurements include 1/4" seam allowances.

From fat quarter #1:
- Cut 1 **outer cover center strip** 17" x 3 1/2".
- Cut 1 **small lining** 8 1/2" x 10 1/2".
- Cut 1 **large lining** 9" x 10 1/2".
- Cut 1 square 4 1/2" x 4 1/2". Cut square in half *once* diagonally to make 1 **tab** and 1 **tab lining**.

From fat quarters #2:
- Cut 2 **outer cover outer strips** 17" x 3 1/2".
- Cut 1 **narrow pocket** 10 1/2" x 3 1/2".
- Cut 1 **pocket** 10 1/2" x 4 1/2".
- Cut 1 **wide pocket** 10 1/2" x 9".
- Cut 2 **corner squares** 3" x 3".

From fat quarter #3 (no cutting diagram given):
- Cut 1 **flap** and 1 **flap lining** 6 1/2" x 10 1/2".
- Cut 2 **outer cover accent strips** 17" x 1".

From fusible woven interfacing:
- Cut 1 **interfacing outer cover** 17" x 10 1/2".
- Cut 1 **interfacing small lining** 8 1/2" x 10 1/2".
- Cut 1 **interfacing large lining** 9" x 10 1/2".
- Cut 1 **interfacing flap** and 1 **interfacing flap lining** 6 1/2" x 10 1/2".
- Cut 1 square 4 1/2" x 4 1/2". Cut square in half *once* diagonally to make 1 **interfacing tab** and 1 **interfacing tab lining**.

From stiff stabilizer:
- Cut 1 **base** 22 1/2" x 10".

Fat Quarter #1

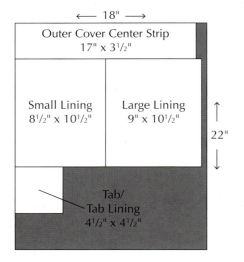

Fat Quarters #2

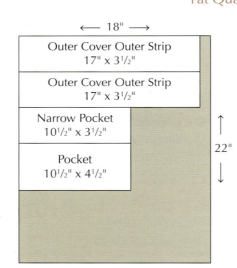

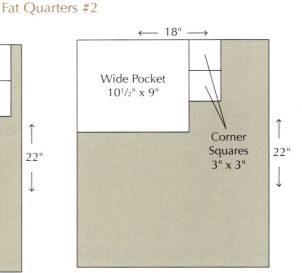

Interfacing

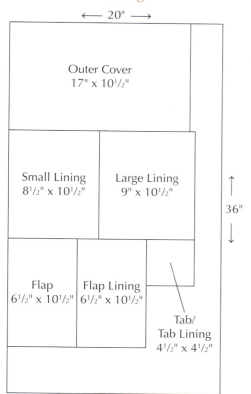

MAKING THE LINING

*Follow **Piecing**, page 63, and **Pressing**, page 64, to make the cover. Use ¼" seam allowances throughout.*

1. Following manufacturer's instructions, fuse each **interfacing lining** piece to wrong side of each corresponding fabric **lining** piece.

2. Fold and press each **corner square** in half diagonally to make 2 **corner triangles** *(Fig. 1)*.

Fig. 1

17

3. Matching raw edges, pin 1 corner triangle to each lower corner of **small lining**. Pin 1 elastic length to each upper corner. Using a scant ¼" seam allowance, baste triangles and elastic lengths to lining *(Fig. 2)*. Trim elastic even with edges of lining.

Fig. 2

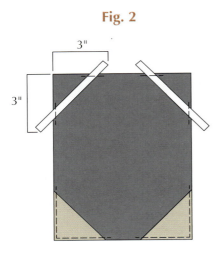

4. For the pocket, match wrong sides and press **narrow pocket**, **pocket**, and wide **pocket** in half lengthwise. Matching raw edges, pin narrow pocket and pocket together *(Fig. 3)*. Spacing as desired (ours are approximately 3½" apart), sew from pocket fold to raw edge to make divided pocket.

Fig. 3

5. Matching raw edges, pin divided pocket and **wide pocket** on left edge of **large lining**. Spacing as desired (ours are approximately 1" apart), sew from wide pocket fold to raw edge to make 2 pencil pockets *(Fig. 4)*. Using a scant ¼" seam allowance, baste pocket to lining along raw edges.

Fig. 4

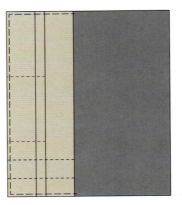

6. Sew **tab** and **tab lining** together along short edges only; clip point, turn right side out and press. Topstitch ¼" from sewn edges. Matching raw edges, center and baste tab to one long edge of **flap lining** *(Fig. 5)*.

Fig. 5

7. Sew large lining, small lining, and **flap lining** together *(Fig. 6)*. Press seams away from small lining. Using fabric marker, draw a line ½" from each seam. Press short raw edge ¼" to the wrong side.

Fig. 6

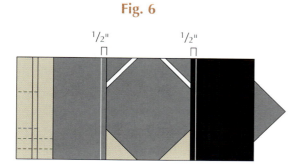

MAKING THE COVER

1. Matching long edges, sew **outer cover outer strips**, **outer cover center strip**, and **outer cover accent strips** together to make **outer cover** *(Fig. 7)*.

Fig. 7

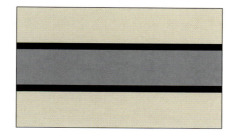

2. Fuse **interfacing flap** and **interfacing outer cover** to wrong side of each corresponding fabric piece.

3. Sew outer cover and **flap** together *(Fig. 8)*. Sew one piece of loop and hook fastener to right side of outer cover. Press short raw edge ¼" to the wrong side.

Fig. 8

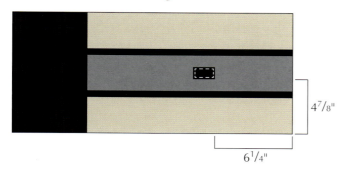

4. Unfolding pressed edges and keeping tab between the layers, sew outer cover and lining together *(Fig. 9)*. Trim seams and clip corners. Turn cover right side out, pushing out curves, corners, and tab with a chopstick or skewer; press.

Fig. 9

5. Slide **base** into cover and align outer seams with edges of base; press. *Note:* It will be a tight fit and you may have to slightly curl the base to slide it into the cover.

6. Stitch in the ditch along the vertical seams. Stitch on drawn lines. Refold pressed edges to the wrong side. Topstitch around entire cover, closing open edges in stitching *(Fig. 10)*.

Fig. 10

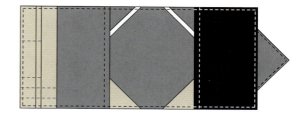

7. Stitching through all layers, sew remaining hook and loop fastener piece to lining side of tab *(Fig. 11)*. Layer and sew buttons to tab.

Fig. 11

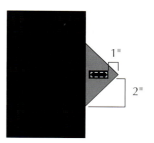

e-Reader
Cover 1

For iPad Mini, Kindle 1, Nook Color, and other tablets measuring approximately 5½" x 8" (14 cm x 20 cm). For this version, a fabric loop buttoned through a large grommet keeps the rounded flap securely closed.

Finished Cover Size (closed): approx. 6" x 8½" x ½" (15 cm x 22 cm x 1 cm)
Finished Cover Size (open): approx. 17½" x 8½" (44 cm x 22 cm)

SHOPPING LIST

Fat quarters are approximately 22" x 18" (56 cm x 46 cm).

- ☐ 2 coordinating fat quarters
- ☐ 4" x 7½" (10 cm x 19 cm) rectangle of fabric for loop
- ☐ ⅝ yd (57 cm) of 20" (51 cm) wide fusible woven interfacing such as Pellon® Shape-Flex® SF 101
- ☐ ⅜ yd (34 cm) of 20" (51 cm) wide sew-in stiff stabilizer such as Pellon® Peltex® 70 Sew-In Ultra Firm Stabilizer
- ☐ 1½" (38 mm) dia. grommet with a 1" (25 mm) dia. opening
- ☐ ⅝" (15 mm) dia. button
- ☐ Removable fabric marking pen or pencil
- ☐ Tracing paper

CUTTING THE PIECES

*Refer to **Cutting Diagrams**, below, to cut fabric. All measurements include ¼" seam allowances. Flap #1 pattern is on page 24.*

From fat quarter #1:
- Cut 1 **outer cover** 13" x 9".
- Cut 4 **corner squares** 2½" x 2½".

From fat quarter #2:
- Cut 1 **flap** and 1 **flap lining** from flap #1 pattern.
- Cut 1 **small lining** 6½" x 9".
- Cut 1 **large lining** 7" x 9".
- Cut 1 **pocket** 6" x 9".

From fusible woven interfacing:
- Cut 1 **interfacing outer cover** 13" x 9".
- Cut 1 **interfacing small lining** 6½" x 9".
- Cut 1 **interfacing large lining** 7" x 9".
- Cut 1 **interfacing flap** and 1 **interfacing flap lining** from flap #1 pattern.

From stiff stabilizer:
- Cut 1 **base** 17½" x 8½".

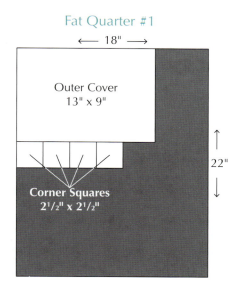

Fat Quarter #1

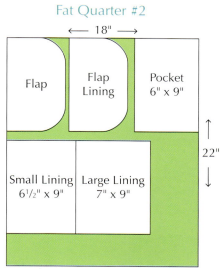

Fat Quarter #2

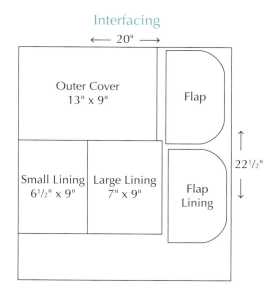

Interfacing

MAKING THE LINING

*Follow **Piecing**, page 63, and **Pressing**, page 64, to make the cover. Use 1/4" seam allowances throughout.*

1. Following manufacturer's instructions, fuse each **interfacing lining** piece to wrong side of each corresponding **lining** piece.

2. Fold and press each **corner square** in half diagonally to make 4 **corner triangles** *(Fig. 1)*.

Fig. 1

3. Matching raw edges, pin 1 corner triangle to each corner of **small lining**. Using a scant 1/4" seam allowance baste corner triangles to lining *(Fig. 2)*.

Fig. 2

4. For the pocket, match wrong sides and press **pocket** in half lengthwise. Matching raw edges, pin pocket to left edge of **large lining**. Using a scant 1/4" seam allowance, baste pocket to lining along raw edges. Spacing as desired (ours are approximately 1" - 2 1/2" apart), sew from fold to outer edge to divide pocket *(Fig. 3)*.

Fig. 3

22   www.leisurearts.com

5. Sew large lining, small lining, and **flap lining** together *(Fig. 4)*. Press seams away from small lining. Using fabric marker, draw a line ¹⁄₂" from each seam. Press short raw edge ¹⁄₄" to the wrong side.

Fig. 4

MAKING THE COVER

1. Fuse **interfacing outer cover** and **interfacing flap** to wrong side of each corresponding fabric piece.

2. Sew **outer cover** and **flap** together *(Fig. 5)*. Press seams toward outer cover. Press short raw edge ¹⁄₄" to the wrong side.

Fig. 5

3. Unfolding pressed edges, sew outer cover and lining together *(Fig. 6)*. Trim seams and clip curves. Turn cover right side out, pushing out curves with a chopstick or skewer; press.

Fig. 6

4. To shape flap end of **base**, trim flap pattern along dashed lines. Draw around curved edge of pattern on one end of base *(Fig. 7)*; cut along drawn line.

Fig. 7

5. Slide base into cover and align outer seams with edges of base; press. *Note:* It will be a tight fit and you may have to slightly curl the base to slide it into the cover.

6. Stitch in the ditch along the vertical seams. Stitch on drawn lines. Refold pressed edges to the wrong side. Topstitch around entire cover, closing open edges in stitching *(Fig. 8)*.

Fig. 8

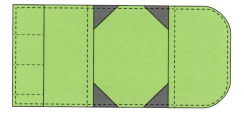

7. Follow manufacturer's instructions to attach grommet to cover as shown in **Fig. 9**.

Fig. 9

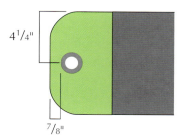

4¹⁄₄"

⁷⁄₈"

8. For loop, press one short edge of **rectangle** 1/4" to the wrong side. Matching wrong sides and long edges, press loop in half. Open and press each long raw edge to center crease *(Fig. 10)*. Re-fold on center crease. Leaving raw edge unsewn, topstitch around loop. Make a buttonhole 1/2" from finished end of loop *(Fig. 11)*.

Fig. 10

Fig. 11

9. Baste raw end of loop to outer cover as shown in **Fig. 12**. Fold loop back over raw end and topstitch across fold *(Fig. 13)*.

Fig. 12

Fig. 13

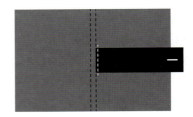

10. Fold cover along stitched lines. Thread loop through grommet and mark button placement on loop. Sew button to loop.

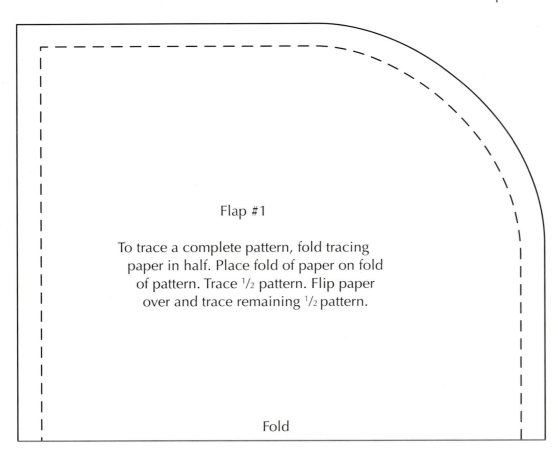

Flap #1

To trace a complete pattern, fold tracing paper in half. Place fold of paper on fold of pattern. Trace 1/2 pattern. Flip paper over and trace remaining 1/2 pattern.

Fold

e-Reader
Cover 2

For iPad Mini, Kindle 1, Nook Color, and other tablets measuring approximately 5½" x 8" (14 cm x 20 cm). This version has a rectangular pieced flap with a triangular tab.

Finished Cover Size (closed): approx. 6" x 8½" x ½" (15 cm x 22 cm x 1 cm)
Finished Cover Size (open): approx. 17½" x 8½" (44 cm x 22 cm)

SHOPPING LIST

Fat quarters are approximately 22" x 18" (56 cm x 46 cm).

- ☐ Fat quarter 1# (floral batik)
- ☐ Fat quarter 2# (blue batik)
- ☐ Fat quarter 3# (gold batik)
- ☐ ⅝ yd (57 cm) of 20" (51 cm) wide fusible woven interfacing such as Pellon® Shape-Flex® SF 101
- ☐ ⅜ yd (34 cm) of 20" (51 cm) wide sew-in stiff stabilizer such as Pellon® Peltex® 70 Sew-In Ultra Firm Stabilizer
- ☐ 1½" (4 cm) of ¾" (19 mm) wide hook and loop fastener
- ☐ 1" (25 mm) dia. button
- ☐ Removable fabric marking pen or pencil

CUTTING THE PIECES

*Refer to **Cutting Diagrams**, below, to cut fabric.
All measurements include ¼" seam allowances.*

From fat quarter #1:
- Cut 1 **outer cover** 13" x 9".
- Cut 1 **wide flap strip** 1¾" x 9".
- Cut 1 **flap strip** 1¼" x 9".
- Cut 4 **corner squares** 2½" x 2½".

From fat quarter #2:
- Cut 1 **flap lining** 5½" x 9".
- Cut 1 **small lining** 6½" x 9".
- Cut 1 **large lining** 7" x 9".
- Cut 1 **strip B** 2" x 9".
- Cut 1 **narrow pocket** 3½" x 9".
- Cut 1 **pocket** 4½" x 9".
- Cut 2 **narrow flap strips** 1" x 9".
- Cut 1 square 3⅞" x 3⅞". Cut square in half *once* diagonally to make 1 **tab** and 1 **tab lining**.

From fat quarter #3:
- Cut 2 **strip A's** 2" x 9".
- Cut 1 **wide pocket** 8½" x 9".
- Cut 1 square 2½" x 2½". Cut square in half once diagonally to make 2 **corner triangles**.

From fusible woven interfacing:
- Cut 1 **interfacing outer cover** 13" x 9".
- Cut 1 **interfacing small lining** 6½" x 9".
- Cut 1 **interfacing large lining** 7" x 9".
- Cut 1 **interfacing flap** and 1 **interfacing flap lining** 5½" x 9".
- Cut 1 square 3⅞" x 3⅞". Cut square in half *once* diagonally to make 1 **interfacing tab** and 1 **interfacing tab lining**.

From stiff stabilizer:
- Cut 1 **base** 17½" x 8½".

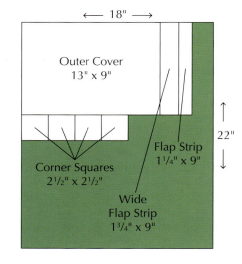

Fat Quarter #1

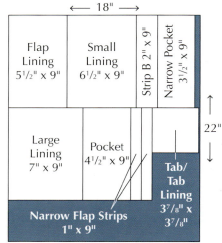

Fat Quarter #2

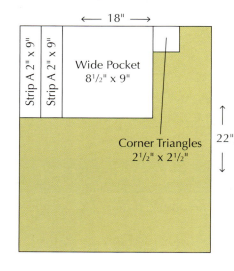

Fat Quarter #3

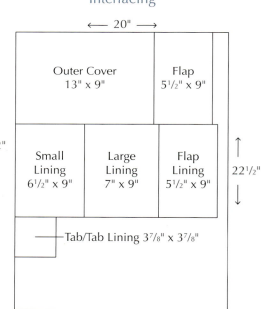

Interfacing

MAKING THE LINING

*Follow **Piecing**, page 63, and **Pressing**, page 64, to make the cover. Use ¼" seam allowances throughout.*

1. Following manufacturer's instructions, fuse each **interfacing lining** piece to wrong side of each corresponding **lining** piece.

2. Fold and press each **corner square** in half diagonally to make 4 **corner triangles** *(Fig. 1)*.

Fig. 1

3. Matching raw edges, pin 1 corner triangle to each corner of **small lining**. Using a scant ¼" seam allowance, sew corner triangles to lining *(Fig. 2)*.

Fig. 2

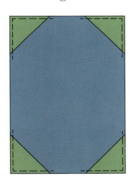

4. For the pocket, match wrong sides and press **narrow pocket**, **pocket**, and **wide pocket** in half lengthwise. Matching raw edges, layer pockets. Spacing as desired (ours are approximately 3½" apart), sew from pocket fold to raw edge to divide pocket *(Fig. 3)*.

Fig. 3

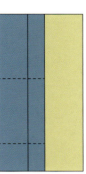

5. Matching raw edges, pin pocket on left edge of **large lining**. Spacing as desired (ours is approximately 1" wide), sew from wide pocket fold to raw edge to make a pencil pocket. Using a scant ¼" seam allowance, baste pocket to lining along raw edges *(Fig. 4)*.

Fig. 4

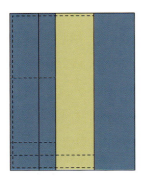

6. Sew large lining, small lining, and **flap lining** together *(Fig. 5)*. Press seams away from small lining. Using fabric marker, draw a line ½" from each seam. Press short raw edge ¼" to the wrong side.

Fig. 5

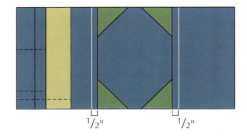

MAKING THE COVER

1. For flap, sew 2 strip A's and strip B together to make **Strip Set**. Cut across **Strip Set** at 2" intervals to make 4 **Unit 1's**.

Strip Set   **Unit 1** (make 4)

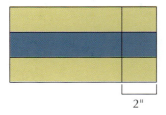 

2. Offsetting units as shown, sew 4 Unit 1's and 2 **corner triangles** together to make **Unit 2**. Leaving a ¼" seam allowance at points, trim Unit 2 to 2½" x 9" *(Fig. 6)*.

Unit 2

Fig. 6

3. Sew 1 **narrow flap strip** and **wide flap strip** to one long edge of Unit 2. Sew 1 narrow flap strip and **flap strip** to opposite edge to make **flap**.

Flap

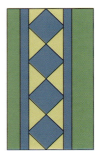

4. Fuse **interfacing flap** and **interfacing outer cover** to wrong side of each corresponding fabric piece.

5. For tab, sew **tab** and **tab lining** together along 2 short edges. Clip corner and turn to the right side; press. Topstitch along finished edges.

Tab

6. Matching raw edges, center and baste tab to narrow strip edge of flap *(Fig. 7)*.

Fig. 7

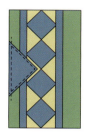

7. Sew **outer cover** and flap together *(Fig. 8)*. Press seams toward outer cover. Sew one piece of hook and loop fastener to right side of outer cover. Press short raw edge $1/4$" to the wrong side.

Fig. 8

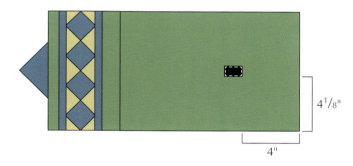

8. Unfolding pressed edges and keeping tab between the layers, sew outer cover and lining together *(Fig. 9)*. Trim seams and clip corners. Turn cover right side out, pushing out corners and tab with a chopstick or skewer; press.

Fig. 9

9. Slide **base** into cover and align seams with edges of base; press. *Note:* It will be a tight fit and you may have to slightly curl the base to slide it into the cover.

10. Stitch in the ditch along the vertical seams. Stitch on drawn lines. Refold pressed edges to the wrong side. Topstitch around entire cover, closing open edges in stitching *(Fig. 10)*.

Fig. 10

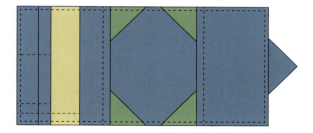

11. Stitching through all layers, sew remaining hook and loop fastener piece to lining side of flap where indicated in **Fig. 11**. Sew button to right side of tab.

Fig. 11

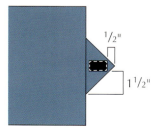

e-Reader
Cover 3

For iPad Mini, Kindle 1, Nook Color, and other tablets measuring approximately 5$\frac{1}{2}$" x 8" (14 cm x 20 cm). This version features a contrasting asymmetrical curved flap embellished with layered buttons.

Finished Cover Size (closed): approx. 6" x 8$\frac{1}{2}$" x $\frac{1}{2}$" (15 cm x 22 cm x 1 cm)
Finished Cover Size (open): approx. 17$\frac{1}{2}$" x 8$\frac{1}{2}$" (44 cm x 22 cm)

SHOPPING LIST

Fat quarters are approximately 22" x 18" (56 cm x 46 cm).

- ☐ 2 coordinating fat quarters
- ☐ $\frac{5}{8}$ yd (57 cm) of 20" (51 cm) wide fusible woven interfacing such as Pellon® Shape-Flex® SF 101
- ☐ $\frac{3}{8}$ yd (34 cm) of 20" (51 cm) wide sew-in stiff stabilizer such as Pellon® Peltex® 70 Sew-In Ultra Firm Stabilizer
- ☐ 1$\frac{1}{2}$" (4 cm) of $\frac{3}{4}$" (19 mm) wide hook and loop fastener
- ☐ 1$\frac{3}{4}$" (44 mm) dia. button
- ☐ 1" (25 mm) dia. button
- ☐ Removable fabric marking pen or pencil

CUTTING THE PIECES

*Refer to **Cutting Diagrams**, below, to cut fabric. All measurements include 1/4" seam allowances. Flap #3 pattern is on page 33.*

From fat quarter #1:
- Cut 1 **outer cover** 13" x 9".
- Cut 4 **corner squares** 2 1/2" x 2 1/2".
- Cut 1 **pocket** 6" x 9".

From fat quarter #2:
- Cut 1 **flap** and 1 **flap lining reversed** from flap #3 pattern.
- Cut 1 **small lining** 6 1/2" x 9".
- Cut 1 **large lining** 7" x 9".

From fusible woven interfacing:
- Cut 1 **interfacing outer cover** 13" x 9".
- Cut 1 **interfacing small lining** 6 1/2" x 9".
- Cut 1 **interfacing large lining** 7" x 9".
- Cut 1 **interfacing flap** and 1 **interfacing flap lining reversed** from flap #3 pattern.

From stiff stabilizer:
- Cut 1 **base** 17 1/2" x 8 1/2".

MAKING THE LINING

*Follow **Piecing**, page 63, and **Pressing**, page 64, to make the cover. Use 1/4" seam allowances throughout.*

1. Following manufacturer's instructions, fuse each **interfacing lining** piece to wrong side of each corresponding **lining** piece.

2. Fold and press each **corner square** in half diagonally to make 4 **corner triangles** *(Fig. 1)*.

Fig. 1

3. Matching raw edges, pin 1 corner triangle to each corner of **small lining**. Using a scant 1/4" seam allowance, sew corner triangles to lining *(Fig. 2)*.

Fig. 2

Fat Quarter #1

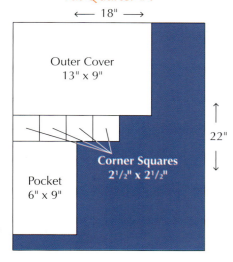

Fat Quarter #2

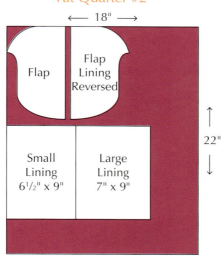

Interfacing

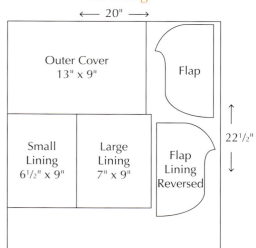

4. For the pocket, match wrong sides and press **pocket** in half lengthwise. Matching raw edges, pin pocket to left edge of **large lining**. Using a scant ¼" seam allowance, baste pocket to lining along raw edges. Spacing as desired (ours are approximately 1" - 2½" apart), sew from fold to outer edge to divide pocket *(Fig. 3)*.

Fig. 3

5. Sew large lining, small lining, and **flap lining** together *(Fig. 4)*. Press seams away from small lining. Using fabric marker, draw a line ½" from each seam. Press short raw edge ¼" to the wrong side.

Fig. 4

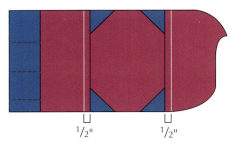

MAKING THE COVER

1. Fuse **interfacing outer cover** and **interfacing flap** to wrong side of each corresponding fabric piece.

2. Sew **outer cover** and **flap** together *(Fig. 5)*. Press seams toward outer cover. Sew one piece of hook and loop fastener to right side of outer cover. Press short raw edge ¼" to the wrong side.

Fig. 5

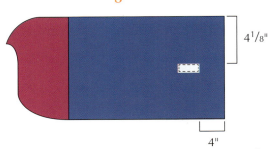

3. Unfolding pressed edges, sew outer cover and lining together *(Fig. 6)*. Trim seams and clip curves and point. Turn cover right side out, pushing out curves and point with a chopstick or skewer; press.

Fig. 6

4. To shape flap end of **base**, trim flap pattern along dashed lines. Draw around curved edge of pattern on one end of base *(Fig. 7)*; cut along drawn line.

Fig. 7

32   www.leisurearts.com

5. Slide base into cover and align seams with edges of base; press. **Note:** It will be a tight fit and you may have to slightly curl the base to slide it into the cover.

6. Stitch in the ditch along the vertical seams. Stitch on drawn lines. Refold pressed edges to the wrong side. Topstitch around entire cover, closing open edges in stitching *(Fig. 8)*.

Fig. 8

7. Stitching through all layers, sew remaining hook and loop fastener piece to lining side of flap where indicated in **Fig. 9**. Layer and sew buttons to right side of flap.

Fig. 9

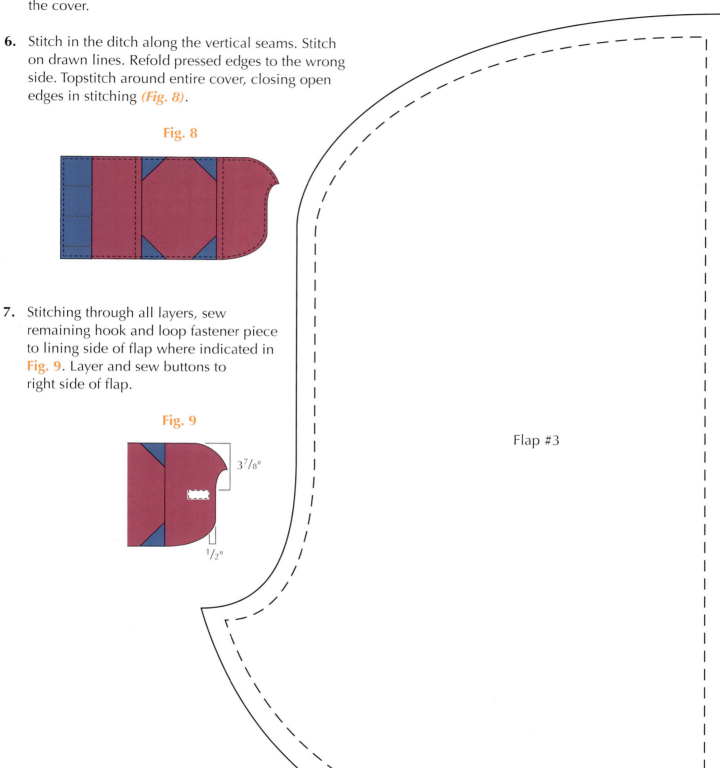

Flap #3

$3 \, ^7/_8"$

$^1/_2"$

Small e-Reader
Cover 1

For Kindle Fire, Kindle Keyboard, Nook HD and other tablets measuring approximately 5" x 7½" (13 cm x 19 cm). This version features a pieced cover and a triangular tab.

Finished Cover Size (closed): approx. 5½" x 8" x ½" (14 cm x 20 cm x 1 cm)
Finished Cover Size (open): approx. 16" x 8" (41 cm x 20 cm)

SHOPPING LIST

Fat quarters are approximately 22" x 18" (56 cm x 46 cm).

- ☐ 2 coordinating fat quarters
- ☐ 5/8 yd (57 cm) of 20" (51 cm) wide fusible woven interfacing such as Pellon® Shape-Flex® SF 101
- ☐ 1/4 yd (23 cm) of 20" (51 cm) wide sew-in stiff stabilizer such as Pellon® Peltex® 70 Sew-In Ultra Firm Stabilizer
- ☐ 1 1/2" (4 cm) of 3/4" (19 mm) wide hook and loop fastener
- ☐ 1 1/8" (29 mm) dia. button
- ☐ Removable fabric marking pen or pencil

CUTTING THE PIECES

*Refer to **Cutting Diagrams**, below, to cut fabric. All measurements include 1/4" seam allowances.*

From fat quarter #1:
- Cut 1 **wide strip** 6" x 18".
- Cut 1 **strip** 1 1/2" x 18".
- Cut 1 **narrow strip** 1" x 18".
- Cut 4 **corner squares** 2 1/2" x 2 1/2".
- Cut 1 **narrow pocket** 3 1/2" x 8 1/2".
- Cut 1 **pocket** 4 1/2" x 8 1/2".
- Cut 1 **wide pocket** 8 1/2" x 8 1/2".

From fat quarter #2:
- Cut 2 **narrow strips** 1" x 18".
- Cut 2 **short narrow strips** 1" x 8 1/2".
- Cut 1 **flap lining** from flap 5" x 8 1/2".
- Cut 1 **small lining** 6" x 8 1/2".
- Cut 1 **large lining** 6 1/2" x 8 1/2".
- Cut 1 square 3 7/8" x 3 7/8". Cut square in half *once* diagonally to make 1 **tab** and 1 **tab lining**.

From fusible woven interfacing:
- Cut 1 **interfacing Unit 4** 12" x 8 1/2".
- Cut 1 **interfacing small lining** 6" x 8 1/2".
- Cut 1 **interfacing large lining** 6 1/2" x 8 1/2".
- Cut 1 **interfacing flap** and 1 **interfacing flap lining** 5" x 8 1/2".
- Cut 1 square 3 7/8" x 3 7/8". Cut square in half *once* diagonally to make 1 **interfacing tab** and 1 **interfacing tab lining**.

From stiff stabilizer:
- Cut 1 **base** 16" x 8".

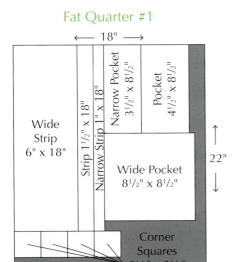

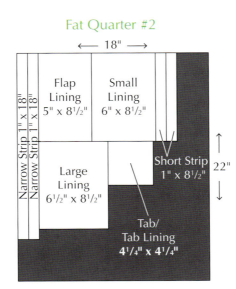

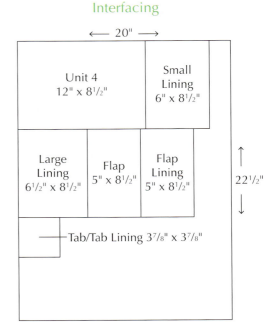

MAKING THE LINING

*Follow **Piecing**, page 63, and **Pressing**, page 64, to make the cover. Use ¼" seam allowances throughout.*

1. Following manufacturer's instructions, fuse each **interfacing lining** piece to wrong side of each corresponding **lining** piece.

2. Fold and press each **corner square** in half diagonally to make 4 **corner triangles** *(Fig. 1)*.

Fig. 1

3. Matching raw edges, pin 1 corner triangle to each corner of **small lining**. Using a scant ¼" seam allowance, sew corner triangles to lining *(Fig. 2)*.

Fig. 2

4. For the pocket, match wrong sides and press **narrow pocket**, **pocket**, and **wide pocket** in half lengthwise. Matching raw edges, pin narrow pocket and pocket together *(Fig. 3)*. To divide pocket, make stitching lines as desired from fold to outer edge of pocket (ours are 1/2", 4", and 4 1/4" from each edge).

Fig. 3

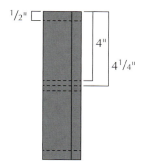

5. Matching raw edges, pin divided pocket and wide pocket on left edge of **large lining** *(Fig. 4)*. Using a scant 1/4" seam allowance, baste pocket to lining along raw edges.

Fig. 4

6. Sew **tab** and **tab lining** together along short edges only; clip point, turn right side out and press. Topstitch 1/4" from sewn edges. Matching raw edges, center and baste tab to one long edge of **flap lining** *(Fig. 5)*.

Fig. 5

7. Sew large lining, small lining, and **flap lining** together *(Fig. 6)*. Press seams away from small lining. Using fabric marker, draw a line 1/2" from each seam. Press short raw edge 1/4" to the wrong side.

Fig. 6

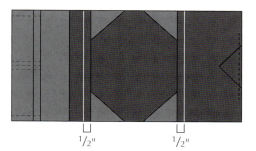

37

MAKING THE COVER

1. Sew **wide strip**, **strip**, and **narrow strips** together to make **Strip Set**. Cut across Strip Set where indicated to make **Unit 1**, **Unit 2**, **Unit 3**, and **Unit 4**.

Strip Set

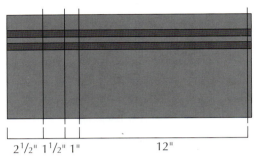

Unit 1

Unit 2

Unit 3

Unit 4

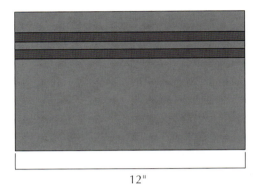

2. Sew Unit's 1, 2, 3, and **short narrow strips** together to make **flap**.

Flap

3. Fuse **interfacing flap** and **interfacing Unit 4** to wrong side of each corresponding fabric piece.

4. Sew Unit 4 and **flap** together to make **outer cover** *(Fig. 7)*. Sew one piece of hook and loop fastener to right side of outer cover. Press Unit 4 short raw edge ¼" to the wrong side.

Fig. 7

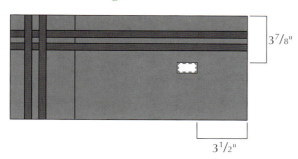

5. Unfolding pressed edges and keeping tab between the layers, sew outer cover and lining together *(Fig. 8)*. Trim seams and clip corners. Turn cover right side out, pushing out corners and tab with a chopstick or skewer; press.

Fig. 8

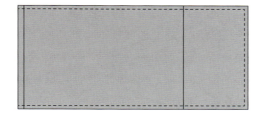

6. Slide **base** into cover and align outer seams with edges of base; press. *Note:* It will be a tight fit and you may have to slightly curl the base to slide it into cover.

7. Stitch in the ditch along the vertical seams. Stitch on drawn lines *(Fig. 9)*. Refold pressed edges to the wrong side. Handstitch opening closed.

Fig. 9

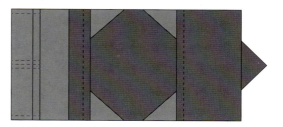

8. Stitching through all layers, sew remaining hook and loop fastener piece to lining side of flap where indicated in **Fig. 10**. Layer and sew buttons to tab.

Fig. 10

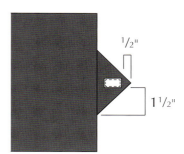

Small e-Reader
Cover 2

For Kindle Fire, Kindle Keyboard, Nook HD and other tablets measuring approximately 5" x 7½" (13 cm x 19 cm). This version features an asymmetrical curved flap embellished with buttons.

Finished Cover Size (closed): approx. 5½" x 8" x ½" (14 cm x 20 cm x 1 cm)
Finished Cover Size (open): approx. 16" x 8" (41 cm x 20 cm)

SHOPPING LIST

Fat quarters are approximately 22" x 18" (56 cm x 46 cm).

- ☐ 2 coordinating fat quarters
- ☐ ⅝ yd (57 cm) of 20" (51 cm) wide fusible woven interfacing such as Pellon® Shape-Flex® SF 101
- ☐ ¼ yd (23 cm) of 20" (51 cm) wide sew-in stiff stabilizer such as Pellon® Peltex® 70 Sew-In Ultra Firm Stabilizer
- ☐ 1½" (4 cm) of ¾" (19 mm) wide hook and loop fastener
- ☐ Five ⅝" (16 mm) dia. buttons
- ☐ Removable fabric marking pen or pencil

CUTTING THE PIECES

*Refer to **Cutting Diagrams**, below, to cut fabric. All measurements include ¼" seam allowances. Flap #2 pattern is on page 43.*

From fat quarter #1:
- Cut 1 **outer cover** 12" x 8½".
- Cut 4 **corner squares** 2½" x 2½".
- Cut 1 **pocket** 6" x 8½".

From fat quarter #2:
- Cut 1 **flap** and 1 **flap lining** from flap #2 pattern.
- Cut 1 **small lining** 6" x 8½".
- Cut 1 **large lining** 6½" x 8½".

From fusible woven interfacing:
- Cut 1 **interfacing outer cover** 12" x 8½".
- Cut 1 **interfacing small lining** 6" x 8½".
- Cut 1 **interfacing large lining** 6½" x 8½".
- Cut 1 **interfacing flap** and **1 interfacing flap lining** from flap #2 pattern.

From stiff stabilizer:
- Cut 1 **base** 16" x 8".

MAKING THE LINING

*Follow **Piecing**, page 63, and **Pressing**, page 64, to make the cover. Use ¼" seam allowances throughout.*

1. Following manufacturer's instructions, fuse each **interfacing lining** piece to wrong side of each corresponding **lining** piece.

2. Fold and press each **corner square** in half diagonally to make 4 **corner triangles** *(Fig. 1)*.

Fig. 1

3. Matching raw edges, pin 1 corner triangle to each corner of **small lining**. Using a scant ¼" seam allowance, sew corner triangles to lining *(Fig. 2)*.

Fig. 2

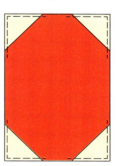

Fat Quarter #1

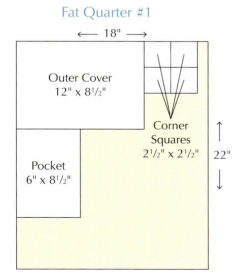

Fat Quarter #2

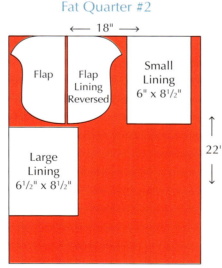

Interfacing

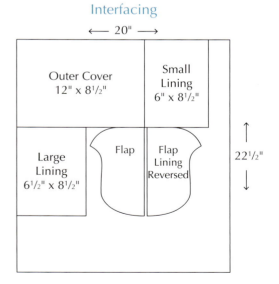

4. For the pocket, match wrong sides and press **pocket** in half lengthwise. Matching raw edges, pin pocket to left edge of **large lining**. Using a scant ¼" seam allowance, baste pocket to lining along three outer edges. Spacing as desired (ours are approximately 2¼" and 1" apart), sew from fold to outer edge to divide pocket *(Fig. 3)*.

Fig. 3

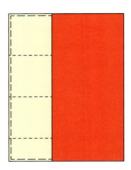

5. Sew large lining, small lining, and **flap lining** together *(Fig. 4)*. Using fabric marker, draw a line ½" from each seam. Press short raw edge ¼" to the wrong side.

Fig. 4

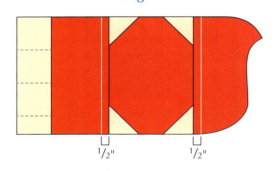

MAKING THE COVER

1. Fuse **interfacing flap** and **interfacing outer cover** to wrong side of each corresponding fabric piece.

2. Sew **outer cover** and **flap** together *(Fig. 5)*. Sew one piece of loop and hook fastener to right side of outer cover. Press short raw edge ¼" to the wrong side.

Fig. 5

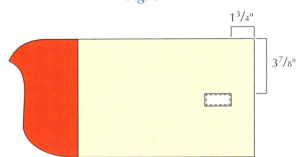

3. Unfolding pressed edges, sew outer cover and lining together *(Fig. 6)*. Trim seams and clip curves and point. Turn cover right side out, pushing out curves and point with a chopstick or skewer; press.

Fig. 6

4. To shape flap end of **base**, trim flap pattern along dashed lines. Draw around curved edge of pattern on one end of base *(Fig. 7)*; cut along drawn line.

Fig. 7

5. Slide base into cover and align outer seams with edges of base; press. *Note:* It will be a tight fit and you may have to slightly curl the base to slide it into the cover.

6. Stitch in the ditch along the vertical seams. Stitch on drawn lines. Refold pressed edges to the wrong side. Topstitch around entire cover, closing open edges in stitching *(Fig. 8)*.

Fig. 8

7. Stitching through all layers, sew remaining hook and loop fastener piece to lining side of flap where indicated in **Fig. 9**. Spacing as desired, sew buttons to right side of flap.

Fig. 9

$3^{5}/_{8}"$

$1/2"$

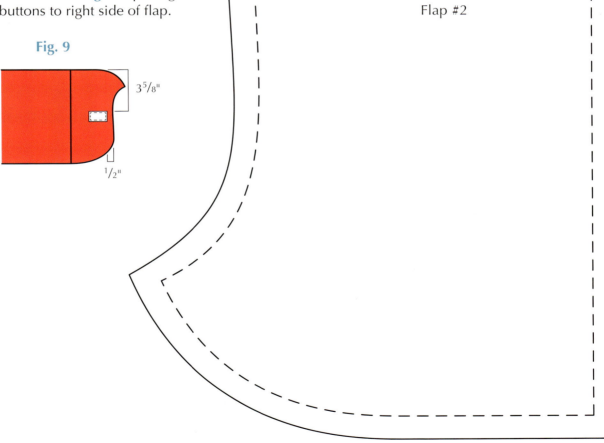

Flap #2

Small e-Reader
Cover 3

For Kindle Fire, Kindle Keyboard, Nook HD and other tablets measuring approximately 5" x 7½" (13 cm x 19 cm). This version features a rounded-edge flap embellished with layered buttons.

Finished Cover Size (closed): approx. 5½" x 8" x ½" (14 cm x 20 cm x 1 cm)
Finished Cover Size (open): approx. 16" x 8" (41 cm x 20 cm)

SHOPPING LIST

Fat quarters are approximately 22" x 18" (56 cm x 46 cm).

- ☐ 2 coordinating fat quarters
- ☐ ⅝ yd (57 cm) of 20" (51 cm) wide fusible woven interfacing such as Pellon® Shape-Flex® SF 101
- ☐ ¼ yd (23 cm) of 20" (51 cm) wide sew-in stiff stabilizer such as Pellon® Peltex® 70 Sew-In Ultra Firm Stabilizer
- ☐ 1½" (4 cm) of ¾" (19 mm) wide hook and loop fastener
- ☐ 2⅛" (54 mm) dia. button
- ☐ 1⅛" (29 mm) dia. button
- ☐ Removable fabric marking pen or pencil
- ☐ Tracing paper

CUTTING THE PIECES

*Refer to **Cutting Diagrams**, below, to cut fabric. All measurements include ¼" seam allowances. Flap pattern #3 is on page 47.*

From fat quarter #1:
- Cut 1 **outer cover** 12" x 8½".

From fat quarter #2:
- Cut 1 **flap** and 1 **flap lining** from flap #3 pattern.
- Cut 1 **small lining** 6" x 8½".
- Cut 1 **large lining** 6½" x 8½".
- Cut 4 **corner squares** 2½" x 2½".
- Cut 1 **pocket** 6" x 8½" (optional).

From fusible woven interfacing:
- Cut 1 **interfacing outer cover** 12" x 8½".
- Cut 1 **interfacing small lining** 6" x 8½".
- Cut 1 **interfacing large lining** 6½" x 8½".
- Cut 1 **interfacing flap** and **1 interfacing flap lining** from flap #3 pattern.

From stiff stabilizer:
- Cut 1 **base** 16" x 8.

MAKING THE LINING

*Follow **Piecing**, page 63, and **Pressing**, page 64, to make the cover. Use ¼" seam allowances throughout.*

1. Following manufacturer's instructions, fuse each **interfacing lining** piece to wrong side of each corresponding **lining** piece.

2. Fold and press each **corner square** in half diagonally to make 4 **corner triangles** *(Fig. 1)*.

Fig. 1

3. Matching raw edges, pin 1 corner triangle to each corner of **small lining**. Using a scant ¼" seam allowance, sew corner triangles to lining *(Fig. 2)*.

Fig. 2

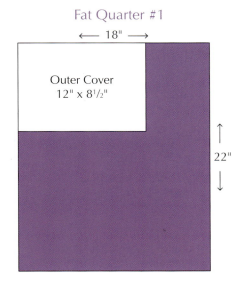

Fat Quarter #1

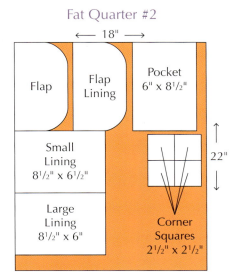

Fat Quarter #2

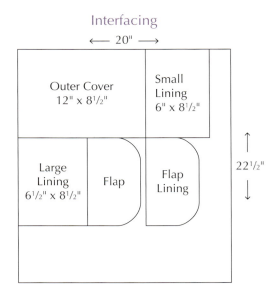

Interfacing

4. For the optional pocket, match wrong sides and press **pocket** in half lengthwise. Matching raw edges, pin pocket to left edge of **large lining**. Using a scant 1/4" seam allowance, baste pocket to lining along three outer edges. Spacing as desired, sew from fold to outer edge to divide pocket *(Fig. 3)*.

Fig. 3

5. Sew large lining, small lining, and **flap lining** together *(Fig. 4)*. Press seams away from small lining. Using fabric marker, draw a line 1/2" from each seam. Press short raw edge 1/4" to the wrong side.

Fig. 4

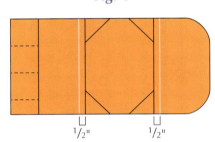

MAKING THE COVER

1. Fuse **interfacing flap** and **interfacing outer cover** to wrong side of each corresponding fabric piece.

2. Sew **outer cover** and **flap** together *(Fig. 5)*. Sew one piece of loop and hook fastener to right side of outer cover. Press short raw edge 1/4" to the wrong side.

Fig. 5

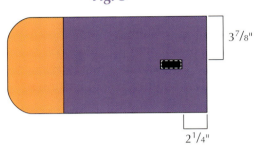

3. Unfolding pressed edges, sew outer cover and lining together *(Fig. 6)*. Trim seams and clip curves. Turn cover right side out, pushing out curves with a chopstick or skewer; press.

Fig. 6

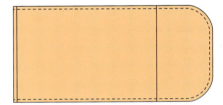

4. To shape flap end of **base**, trim flap pattern along dashed lines. Draw around curved edge of pattern on one end of base *(Fig. 7)*; cut along drawn line.

Fig. 7

5. Slide base into cover and align outer seams with edges of base; press. **Note:** It will be a tight fit and you may have to slightly curl the base to slide it into the cover.

6. Stitch in the ditch along the vertical seams. Stitch on drawn lines. Refold pressed edges to the wrong side. Topstitch around entire cover, closing open edges in stitching *(Fig. 8)*.

7. Stitching through all layers, sew remaining hook and loop fastener piece to lining side of flap where indicated in *Fig. 9*. Layer and sew buttons to right side of flap.

Fig. 8

Fig. 9

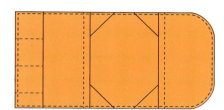

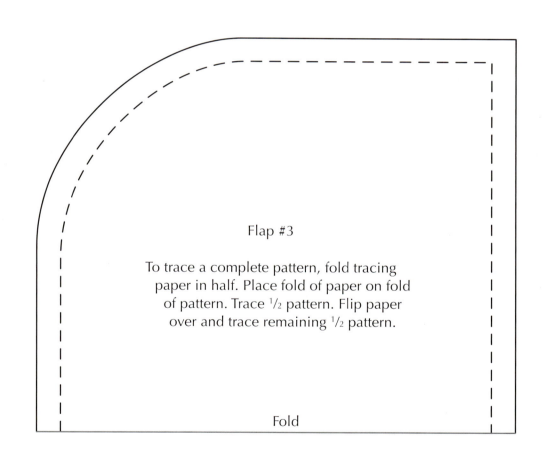

Flap #3

To trace a complete pattern, fold tracing paper in half. Place fold of paper on fold of pattern. Trace $1/2$ pattern. Flip paper over and trace remaining $1/2$ pattern.

Fold

Mini e-Reader
Cover 1

For Kindle Touch, Nook Simple Touch, and other tablets measuring approximately 5" x 6½" (13 cm x 17 cm). This version features an asymmetrical curved flap embellished with a large button.

Finished Cover Size (closed): approx. 5½" x 7" x ½" (14 cm x 18 cm x 1 cm)
Finished Cover Size (open): approx. 15½" x 7" (39 cm x 18 cm)

48 www.leisurearts.com

SHOPPING LIST

Fat quarters are approximately 22" x 18" (56 cm x 46 cm).

- ☐ 2 coordinating fat quarters
- ☐ ½ yd (46 cm) of 20" (51 cm) wide fusible woven interfacing such as Pellon® Shape-Flex® SF 101
- ☐ ¼ yd (23 cm) of 20" (51 cm) wide sew-in stiff stabilizer such as Pellon® Peltex® 70 Sew-In Ultra Firm Stabilizer
- ☐ 1½" (4 cm) of ¾" (19 mm) wide hook and loop fastener
- ☐ 1⅛" (29 mm) dia. button
- ☐ Removable fabric marking pen or pencil

CUTTING THE PIECES

*Refer to **Cutting Diagrams**, below, to cut fabric. All measurements include ¼" seam allowances. Flap pattern #1 is on page 52.*

From fat quarter #1:
- Cut 1 **outer cover** 12" x 7½".
- Cut 4 **corner squares** 2½" x 2½".
- Cut 1 **pocket** 6" x 7½".

From fat quarter #2:
- Cut 1 **flap** and 1 **flap lining reversed** from flap #1 pattern.
- Cut 1 **small lining** 6" x 7½".
- Cut 1 **large lining** 6½" x 7½".

From fusible woven interfacing:
- Cut 1 **interfacing outer cover** 12" x 7½".
- Cut 1 **interfacing small lining** 6" x 7½".
- Cut 1 **interfacing large lining** 6½" x 7½".
- Cut 1 **interfacing flap** and **interfacing flap lining reversed** from flap #1 pattern.

From stiff stabilizer:
- Cut 1 **base** 15½" x 7".

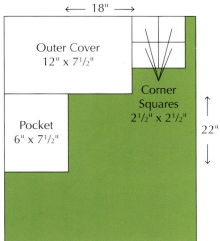

Fat Quarter #1

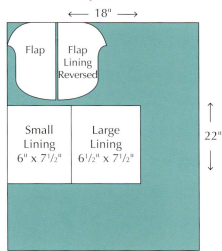

Fat Quarter #2

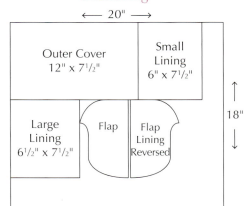

Interfacing

MAKING THE LINING

*Follow **Piecing**, page 63, and **Pressing**, page 64, to make the cover. Use ¼" seam allowances throughout.*

1. Following manufacturer's instructions, fuse each **interfacing lining** piece to wrong side of each corresponding **lining** piece.

2. Fold and press each **corner square** in half diagonally to make 4 **corner triangles** *(Fig. 1)*.

Fig. 1

3. Matching raw edges, pin 1 corner triangle to each corner of **small lining**. Using a scant ¼" seam allowance, sew corner triangles to lining *(Fig. 2)*.

Fig. 2

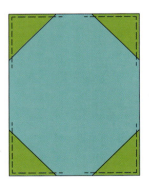

50   www.leisurearts.com

4. For the pocket, match wrong sides and press **pocket** in half lengthwise. Matching raw edges, pin pocket to left edge of **large lining**. Using a scant ¼" seam allowance, baste pocket to lining along three outer edges. Spacing as desired (ours are approximately 2¼" apart), sew from fold to outer edge to divide pocket *(Fig. 3)*.

Fig. 3

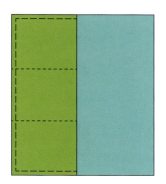

5. Sew large lining, small lining, and **flap lining** together *(Fig. 4)*. Using fabric marker, draw a line ½" from each seam. Press short raw edge ¼" to the wrong side.

Fig. 4

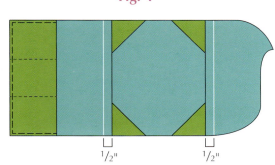

MAKING THE COVER

1. Fuse **interfacing flap** and **interfacing outer cover** to wrong side of each corresponding fabric piece.

2. Sew **outer cover** and **flap** together *(Fig. 5)*. Sew one piece of hook and loop fastener to right side of outer cover. Press short raw edge ¼" to the wrong side.

Fig. 5

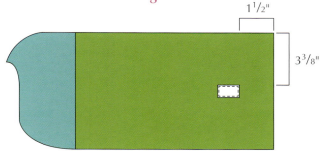

3. Unfolding pressed edges, sew outer cover and lining together *(Fig. 6)*. Trim seams and clip curves and point. Turn cover right side out, pushing out curves and point with a chopstick or skewer; press.

Fig. 6

4. To shape flap end of **base**, trim flap pattern along dashed lines. Draw around curved edge of pattern on one end of base *(Fig. 7)*; cut along drawn line.

Fig. 7

5. Slide base into cover and align outer seams with edges of base; press. *Note:* It will be a tight fit and you may have to slightly curl the base to slide it into cover.

6. Stitch in the ditch along the vertical seams. Stitch on drawn lines. Refold pressed edges to the wrong side. Topstitch around entire cover, closing open edges in stitching *(Fig. 8)*.

Fig. 8

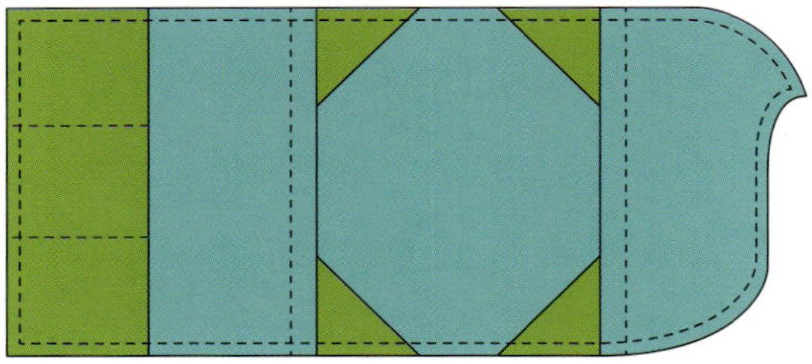

7. Stitching through all layers, sew remaining hook and loop fastener piece to lining side of flap where indicated in **Fig. 9**. Layer and sew buttons to tab.

Fig. 9

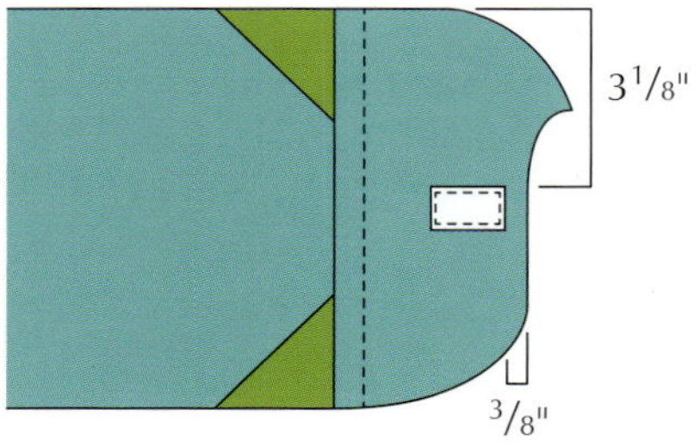

$3^{1}/_{8}"$

$^{3}/_{8}"$

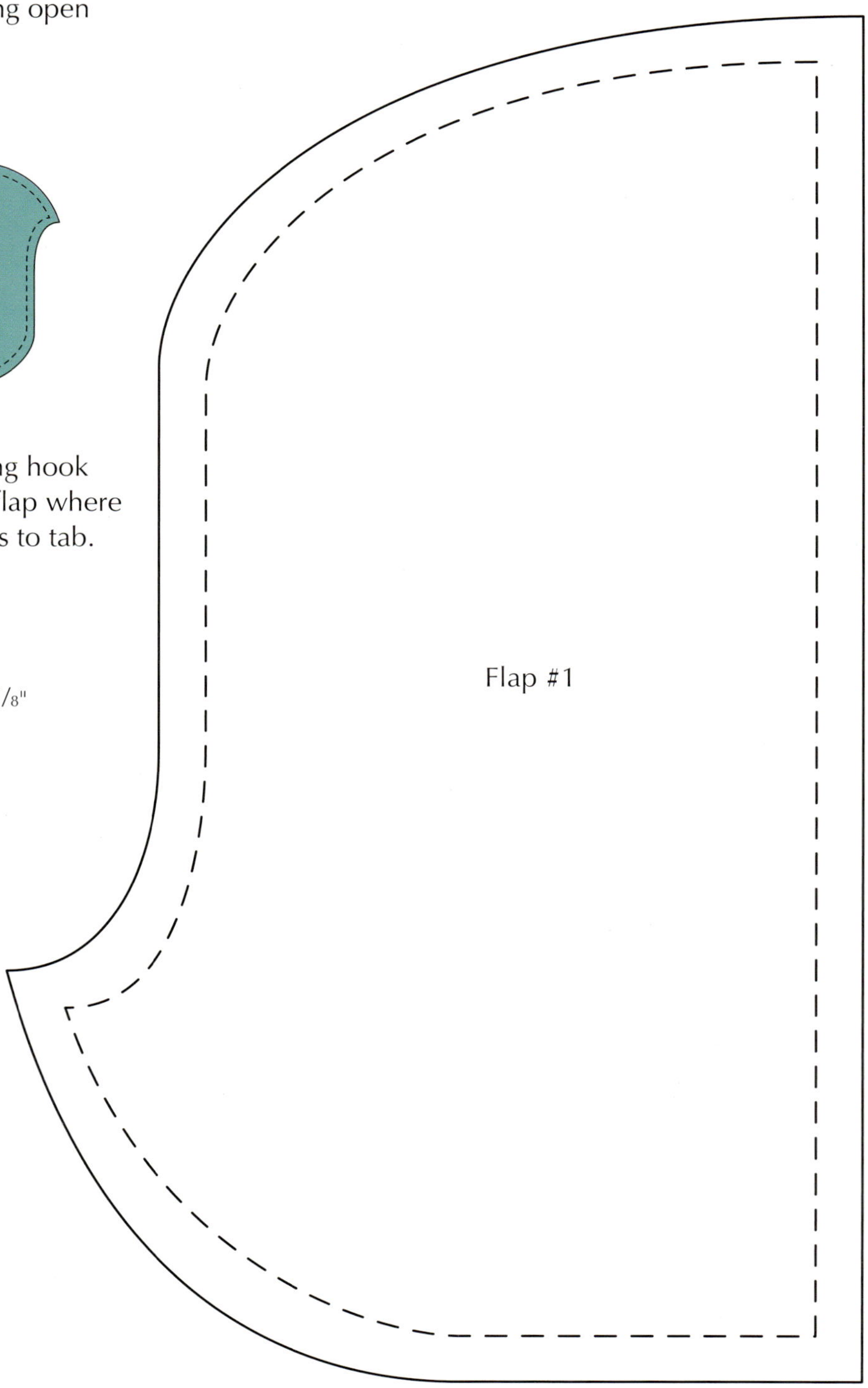

Flap #1

52   www.leisurearts.com

Mini e-Reader
Cover 2

For Kindle Touch, Nook Simple Touch, and other tablets measuring approximately 5" x 6½" (13 cm x 17 cm). For this version, a fabric loop buttoned through a large grommet keeps the rounded flap securely closed.

Finished Cover Size (closed): approx. 5½" x 7" x ½" (14 cm x 18 cm x 1 cm)
Finished Cover Size (open): approx. 15½" x 7" (39 cm x 18 cm)

SHOPPING LIST

Fat quarters are approximately 22" x 18" (56 cm x 46 cm).

- ☐ 1 fat quarter
- ☐ 4" x 6½" (10 cm x 17 cm) rectangle of fabric for loop
- ☐ ½ yd (46 cm) of 20" (51 cm) wide fusible woven interfacing such as Pellon® Shape-Flex® SF 101
- ☐ ¼ yd (23 cm) of 20" (51 cm) wide sew-in stiff stabilizer such as Pellon® Peltex® 70 Sew-In Ultra Firm Stabilizer
- ☐ 1½" (38 mm) dia. grommet with a 1" (25 mm) dia. opening
- ☐ Two ⅝" (15 mm) dia. buttons
- ☐ Removable fabric marking pen or pencil

53

CUTTING THE PIECES

*Refer to **Cutting Diagrams**, right, to cut fabric.
All measurements include ¼" seam allowances.
Flap #2/3 pattern is on page 57.*

From fat quarter:
- Cut 1 **outer cover** 12" x 7½".
- Cut 4 **corner squares** 2½" x 2½".
- Cut 1 **flap** and 1 **flap lining** from flap #2/3 pattern.
- Cut 1 **small lining** 6" x 7½".
- Cut 1 **large lining** 6½" x 7½".
- Cut 1 **pocket** 6" x 7½" (optional).

From fusible woven interfacing:
- Cut 1 **interfacing outer cover** 12" x 7½".
- Cut 1 **interfacing small lining** 6" x 7½".
- Cut 1 **interfacing large lining** 6½" x 7½".
- Cut 1 **interfacing flap** and **interfacing flap lining** from flap #2/3 pattern.

From stiff stabilizer:
- Cut 1 **base** 15½" x 7".

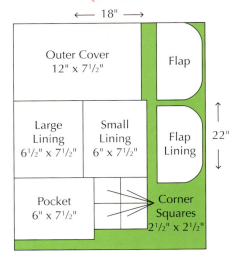

Fat Quarter #1

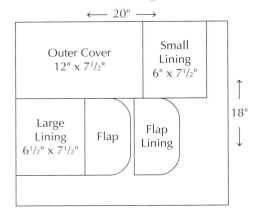

Interfacing

54   www.leisurearts.com

MAKING THE LINING

*Follow **Piecing**, page 63, and **Pressing**, page 64, to make the cover. Use ¼" seam allowances throughout.*

1. Following manufacturer's instructions, fuse each **interfacing lining** piece to wrong side of each corresponding **lining** piece.

2. Fold and press each **corner square** in half diagonally to make 4 **corner triangles** *(Fig. 1)*.

Fig. 1

3. Matching raw edges, pin 1 corner triangle to each corner of **small lining**. Using a scant ¼" seam allowance, sew corner triangles to lining *(Fig. 2)*.

Fig. 2

4. For optional pocket, match wrong sides and press **pocket** in half lengthwise. Matching raw edges, pin pocket to left edge of **large lining**. Using a scant ¼" seam allowance, baste pocket to lining along three outer edges. Spacing as desired, sew from fold to outer edge to divide pocket *(Fig. 3)*.

Fig. 3

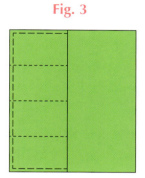

5. Sew large lining, small lining, and **flap lining** together *(Fig. 4)*. Using fabric marker, draw a line ½" from each seam. Press short raw edge ¼" to the wrong side.

Fig. 4

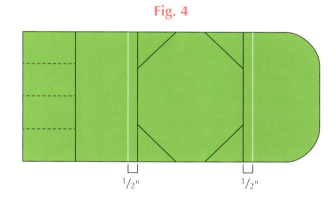

55

MAKING THE COVER

1. Fuse **interfacing flap** and **interfacing outer cover** to wrong side of each corresponding fabric piece.

2. Sew **outer cover** and **flap** together *(Fig. 5)*. Press seams toward outer cover. Press short raw edge 1/4" to the wrong side.

Fig. 5

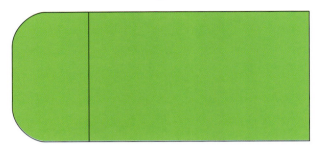

3. Unfolding pressed edges, sew outer cover and lining together *(Fig. 6)*. Trim seams and clip curves. Turn cover right side out, pushing out curves with a chopstick or skewer; press.

Fig. 6

4. To shape flap end of **base**, trim flap pattern along dashed lines. Draw around curved edge of pattern on one end of base *(Fig. 7)*; cut along drawn line.

Fig. 7

5. Slide base into cover and align outer seams with edges of base; press. *Note:* It will be a tight fit and you may have to slightly curl the base to slide it into cover.

6. Stitch in the ditch along the vertical seams. Stitch on drawn lines. Refold pressed edges to the wrong side. Topstitch around entire cover, closing open edges in stitching *(Fig. 8)*.

Fig. 8

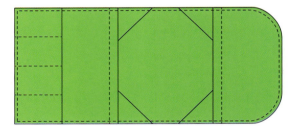

7. Follow manufacturer's instructions to attach grommet to cover as shown in **Fig. 9**.

Fig. 9

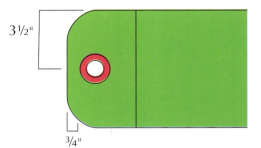

56   www.leisurearts.com

8. For loop, press one short edge of **rectangle** ¼" to the wrong side. Matching wrong sides and long edges, press loop in half. Open and press each long raw edge to center crease **(Fig. 10)**. Re-fold on center crease. Leaving raw edge unsewn, topstitch around loop. Make a buttonhole ½" from finished end of loop **(Fig. 11)**.

Fig. 10

Fig. 11

9. Baste raw end of loop to cover as shown in **Fig. 12**. Fold loop back over raw end and topstitch across fold **(Fig. 13)**.

Fig. 12

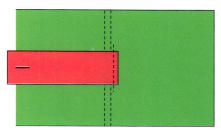

Fig. 13

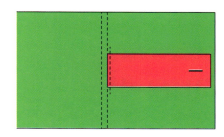

10. Fold cover along stitched lines. Thread loop through grommet and mark button placement on loop. Sew button to loop.

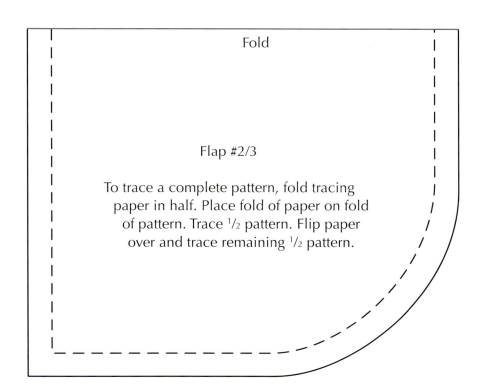

Flap #2/3

To trace a complete pattern, fold tracing paper in half. Place fold of paper on fold of pattern. Trace ½ pattern. Flip paper over and trace remaining ½ pattern.

Mini e-Reader
Cover 3

For Kindle Touch, Nook Simple Touch, and other tablets measuring approximately 5" x 6½" (13 cm x17 cm). This version features a curved flap embellished with layered buttons.

Finished Cover Size (closed): approx. 5½" x 7" x ½" (14 cm x 18 cm x 1 cm)
Finished Cover Size (open): approx. 15½" x 7" (39 cm x 18 cm)

SHOPPING LIST

Fat quarters are approximately 22" x 18" (56 cm x 46 cm).

- ☐ 2 coordinating fat quarters
- ☐ ½ yd (46 cm) of 20" (51 cm) wide fusible woven interfacing such as Pellon® Shape-Flex® SF 101
- ☐ ¼ yd (23 cm) of 20" (51 cm) wide sew-in stiff stabilizer such as Pellon® Peltex® 70 Sew-In Ultra Firm Stabilizer
- ☐ 1½" (4 cm) of ¾" (19 mm) wide hook and loop fastener
- ☐ ¾" (19 mm) dia. button
- ☐ 1½"-2" (38-51 mm) dia. button
- ☐ Removable fabric marking pen or pencil

CUTTING THE PIECES

Refer to Cutting Diagrams, below, to cut fabric. All measurements include ¼" seam allowances. Flap #2/3 pattern is on page 57.

From fat quarter #1:
- Cut 1 **outer cover** 12" x 7½".
- Cut 4 **corner squares** 2½" x 2½".
- Cut 1 **pocket** 6" x 7½".

From fat quarter #2:
- Cut 1 **flap** and 1 **flap lining** from flap #2/3 pattern.
- Cut 1 **small lining** 6" x 7½".
- Cut 1 **large lining** 6½" x 7½".

From fusible woven interfacing:
- Cut 1 **interfacing outer cover** 12" x 7½".
- Cut 1 **interfacing small lining** 6" x 7½".
- Cut 1 **interfacing large lining** 6½" x 7½".
- Cut 1 **interfacing flap** and **interfacing flap lining** from flap #2/3 pattern.

From stiff stabilizer:
- Cut 1 **base** 15½" x 7".

MAKING THE LINING

Follow Piecing, page 63, and Pressing, page 64, to make the cover. Use ¼" seam allowances throughout.

1. Following manufacturer's instructions, fuse each **interfacing lining** piece to wrong side of each corresponding **lining** piece.

2. Fold and press each **corner square** in half diagonally to make 4 **corner triangles** *(Fig. 1)*.

Fig. 1

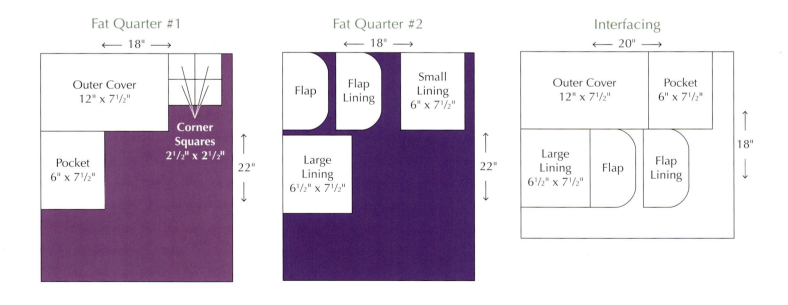

3. Matching raw edges, pin 1 corner triangle to each corner of **small lining**. Using a scant ¼" seam allowance, sew corner triangles to lining *(Fig. 2)*.

Fig. 2

4. For the pocket, match wrong sides and press **pocket** in half lengthwise. Matching raw edges, pin pocket to left edge of **large lining**. Using a scant ¼" seam allowance, baste pocket to lining along three outer edges. Spacing as desired (ours are approximately 2¼" apart), sew from fold to outer edge to divide pocket *(Fig. 3)*.

Fig. 3

5. Sew large lining, small lining, and **flap lining** together *(Fig. 4)*. Using fabric marker, draw a line ½" from each seam. Press short raw edge ¼" to the wrong side.

Fig. 4

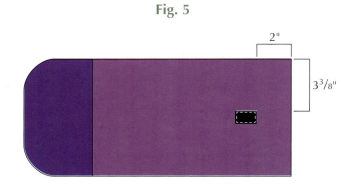

½"   ½"

MAKING THE COVER

1. Fuse **interfacing flap** and **interfacing outer cover** to wrong side of each corresponding fabric piece.

2. Sew **outer cover** and **flap** together *(Fig. 5)*. Sew one piece of hook and loop fastener to right side of outer cover. Press short raw edge ¼" to the wrong side.

Fig. 5

2"

3⅜"

3. Unfolding pressed edges, sew outer cover and lining together *(Fig. 6)*. Trim seams and clip curves. Turn cover right side out, pushing out curves with a chopstick or skewer; press.

Fig. 6

4. To shape flap end of **base**, trim flap pattern along dashed lines. Draw around curved edge of pattern on one end of base *(Fig. 7)*; cut along drawn line.

Fig. 7

5. Slide base into cover and align outer seams with edges of base; press. **Note:** It will be a tight fit and you may have to slightly curl the base to slide it into cover.

6. Stitch in the ditch along the vertical seams. Stitch on drawn lines. Refold pressed edges to the wrong side. Topstitch around entire cover, closing open edges in stitching *(Fig. 8)*.

Fig. 8

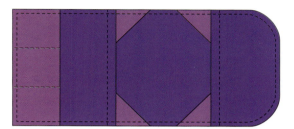

7. Stitching through all layers, sew remaining hook and loop fastener piece to lining side of flap where indicated in **Fig. 9**. Layer and sew buttons to tab.

Fig. 9

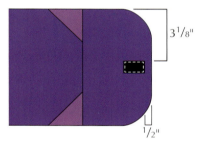

GENERAL INSTRUCTIONS

To make your sewing easier and more enjoyable, we encourage you to carefully read all of the general instructions, study the color photographs, and familiarize yourself with the individual project instructions before beginning a project.

FABRICS

SELECTING FABRICS
Choose high-quality, medium-weight 100% cotton fabric fat quarters.

PREPARING FABRICS
Pre-washing fabrics may cause edges to ravel. As a result, your fat quarters may not be large enough to cut all of the pieces required for your chosen project. Therefore, we **do not** recommend pre-washing.

Before cutting, prepare fabrics with a steam iron set on cotton and starch or sizing. The starch or sizing will give the fabric a crisp finish. This will make cutting more accurate and may make piecing easier.

PIECING

Precise cutting, followed by accurate piecing, will ensure that all pieces of your project fit together well.

- Set sewing machine stitch length for approximately 11 stitches per inch.

- Use neutral-colored general-purpose sewing thread (not quilting thread) in needle and in bobbin.

- An accurate ¼" seam allowance is **essential**. Presser feet that are ¼" wide are available for most sewing machines.

- When piecing, always place pieces right sides together and match raw edges; pin if necessary.

- Trim away points of seam allowances that extend beyond edges of sewn pieces.

SEWING STRIP SETS

When there are several strips to assemble into a strip set, first sew strips together into pairs, then sew pairs together to form strip set. To help avoid distortion, sew seams in opposite directions *(Fig. 1)*.

Fig. 1

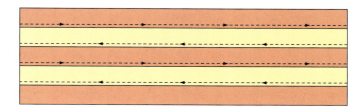

SEWING ACROSS SEAM INTERSECTIONS

When sewing across intersection of two seams, place pieces right sides together and match seams exactly, making sure seam allowances are pressed in opposite directions *(Fig. 2)*.

Fig. 2

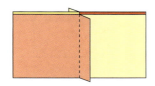

SEWING SHARP POINTS

To ensure sharp points when joining triangular or diagonal pieces, stitch across the center of the "X" (shown in pink) formed on wrong side by previous seams *(Fig. 3)*.

Fig. 3

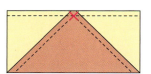

PRESSING

- Use steam iron set on "Cotton" for all pressing.

- Press after sewing each seam.

- Seam allowances are almost always pressed to one side, usually toward darker fabric. However, to reduce bulk it may occasionally be necessary to press seam allowances toward the lighter fabric or even to press them open.

- To prevent dark fabric seam allowance from showing through light fabric, trim darker seam allowance slightly narrower than lighter seam allowance.

Metric Conversion Chart

Inches x 2.54 = centimeters (cm)	Yards x .9144 = meters (m)
Inches x 25.4 = millimeters (mm)	Yards x 91.44 = centimeters (cm)
Inches x .0254 = meters (m)	Centimeters x .3937 = inches (")
	Meters x 1.0936 = yards (yd)

Standard Equivalents

1/8"	3.2 mm	0.32 cm	1/8 yard	11.43 cm	0.11 m
1/4"	6.35 mm	0.635 cm	1/4 yard	22.86 cm	0.23 m
3/8"	9.5 mm	0.95 cm	3/8 yard	34.29 cm	0.34 m
1/2"	12.7 mm	1.27 cm	1/2 yard	45.72 cm	0.46 m
5/8"	15.9 mm	1.59 cm	5/8 yard	57.15 cm	0.57 m
3/4"	19.1 mm	1.91 cm	3/4 yard	68.58 cm	0.69 m
7/8"	22.2 mm	2.22 cm	7/8 yard	80 cm	0.8 m
1"	25.4 mm	2.54 cm	1 yard	91.44 cm	0.91 m

PIECING

Precise cutting, followed by accurate piecing, will ensure that all pieces of your project fit together well.

- Set sewing machine stitch length for approximately 11 stitches per inch.

- Use neutral-colored general-purpose sewing thread (not quilting thread) in needle and in bobbin.

- An accurate 1/4" seam allowance is **essential**. Presser feet that are 1/4" wide are available for most sewing machines.

- When piecing, always place pieces right sides together and match raw edges; pin if necessary.

- Trim away points of seam allowances that extend beyond edges of sewn pieces.

SEWING STRIP SETS

When there are several strips to assemble into a strip set, first sew strips together into pairs, then sew pairs together to form strip set. To help avoid distortion, sew seams in opposite directions *(Fig. 1)*.

Fig. 1

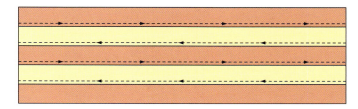

SEWING ACROSS SEAM INTERSECTIONS

When sewing across intersection of two seams, place pieces right sides together and match seams exactly, making sure seam allowances are pressed in opposite directions *(Fig. 2)*.

Fig. 2

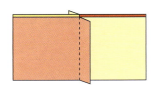

SEWING SHARP POINTS

To ensure sharp points when joining triangular or diagonal pieces, stitch across the center of the "X" (shown in pink) formed on wrong side by previous seams *(Fig. 3)*.

Fig. 3

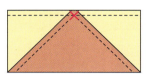

PRESSING

- Use steam iron set on "Cotton" for all pressing.

- Press after sewing each seam.

- Seam allowances are almost always pressed to one side, usually toward darker fabric. However, to reduce bulk it may occasionally be necessary to press seam allowances toward the lighter fabric or even to press them open.

- To prevent dark fabric seam allowance from showing through light fabric, trim darker seam allowance slightly narrower than lighter seam allowance.

Metric Conversion Chart

Inches x 2.54 = centimeters (cm)	Yards x .9144 = meters (m)
Inches x 25.4 = millimeters (mm)	Yards x 91.44 = centimeters (cm)
Inches x .0254 = meters (m)	Centimeters x .3937 = inches (")
	Meters x 1.0936 = yards (yd)

Standard Equivalents

1/8"	3.2 mm	0.32 cm	1/8 yard	11.43 cm	0.11 m
1/4"	6.35 mm	0.635 cm	1/4 yard	22.86 cm	0.23 m
3/8"	9.5 mm	0.95 cm	3/8 yard	34.29 cm	0.34 m
1/2"	12.7 mm	1.27 cm	1/2 yard	45.72 cm	0.46 m
5/8"	15.9 mm	1.59 cm	5/8 yard	57.15 cm	0.57 m
3/4"	19.1 mm	1.91 cm	3/4 yard	68.58 cm	0.69 m
7/8"	22.2 mm	2.22 cm	7/8 yard	80 cm	0.8 m
1"	25.4 mm	2.54 cm	1 yard	91.44 cm	0.91 m

PIECING

Precise cutting, followed by accurate piecing, will ensure that all pieces of your project fit together well.

- Set sewing machine stitch length for approximately 11 stitches per inch.

- Use neutral-colored general-purpose sewing thread (not quilting thread) in needle and in bobbin.

- An accurate ¼" seam allowance is **essential**. Presser feet that are ¼" wide are available for most sewing machines.

- When piecing, always place pieces right sides together and match raw edges; pin if necessary.

- Trim away points of seam allowances that extend beyond edges of sewn pieces.

SEWING STRIP SETS

When there are several strips to assemble into a strip set, first sew strips together into pairs, then sew pairs together to form strip set. To help avoid distortion, sew seams in opposite directions *(Fig. 1)*.

Fig. 1

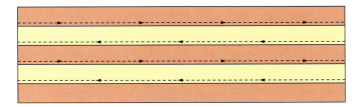

SEWING ACROSS SEAM INTERSECTIONS

When sewing across intersection of two seams, place pieces right sides together and match seams exactly, making sure seam allowances are pressed in opposite directions *(Fig. 2)*.

Fig. 2

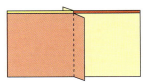

SEWING SHARP POINTS

To ensure sharp points when joining triangular or diagonal pieces, stitch across the center of the "X" (shown in pink) formed on wrong side by previous seams *(Fig. 3)*.

Fig. 3

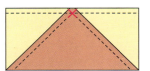

PRESSING

- Use steam iron set on "Cotton" for all pressing.

- Press after sewing each seam.

- Seam allowances are almost always pressed to one side, usually toward darker fabric. However, to reduce bulk it may occasionally be necessary to press seam allowances toward the lighter fabric or even to press them open.

- To prevent dark fabric seam allowance from showing through light fabric, trim darker seam allowance slightly narrower than lighter seam allowance.

Metric Conversion Chart

Inches x 2.54 = centimeters (cm)
Inches x 25.4 = millimeters (mm)
Inches x .0254 = meters (m)

Yards x .9144 = meters (m)
Yards x 91.44 = centimeters (cm)
Centimeters x .3937 = inches (")
Meters x 1.0936 = yards (yd)

Standard Equivalents

1/8"	3.2 mm	0.32 cm	1/8 yard	11.43 cm	0.11 m
1/4"	6.35 mm	0.635 cm	1/4 yard	22.86 cm	0.23 m
3/8"	9.5 mm	0.95 cm	3/8 yard	34.29 cm	0.34 m
1/2"	12.7 mm	1.27 cm	1/2 yard	45.72 cm	0.46 m
5/8"	15.9 mm	1.59 cm	5/8 yard	57.15 cm	0.57 m
3/4"	19.1 mm	1.91 cm	3/4 yard	68.58 cm	0.69 m
7/8"	22.2 mm	2.22 cm	7/8 yard	80 cm	0.8 m
1"	25.4 mm	2.54 cm	1 yard	91.44 cm	0.91 m